INCONCEIVABLE TRUTHS

CODY GILMORE

Dedication

He is the way, strong and steady,

She is willing, determined, and ready.

Hand in hand, they conquer all,

Together, they rise, never to fall.

In her, he finds his guiding light,

In him, her strength takes flight.

The will and the way, a perfect pair,

Love's journey they bravely share.

-CG

About the Author

Drawing from a wealth of experiences, emotions, and personal revelations, Cody Gilmore narrates a tale that spans generations and transcends conventional notions of family and identity.

As the protagonist of his own story, Gilmore grapples with the intricacies of family dynamics as he takes readers on a rollercoaster of emotions, from the challenges of discovering his biological roots to the shocking realization of new relationships.

As readers delve into the pages of Inconceivable Truths, they will undoubtedly be moved by Cody's narrative, resonating with its universal themes of love, forgiveness, and the profound impact of the family we choose.

Cody invites readers to embark on this remarkable journey as they witness the power of love, the strength of bonds, and the transformative nature of self-discovery. Through his writing, Cody leaves an incredible mark on the hearts and minds of readers, reminding us all that amidst life's twists and turns, the pursuit of truth and love ultimately defines our path.

Some of the names in the book have been changed to protect individuals who would prefer to keep this a secret...Which I totally understand.

Author's Note

My name is Cody Gilmore, and *Inconceivable Truths* is the first story I've written. Writing has drawn me in for many years, and I'm excited to finally share my ideas with you. There are many more stories and concepts in my mind, and I can't wait to bring them to life.

I grew up in Tucson, AZ, where my roots run deep. It's where I chose to marry my wife and raise our children. Though I've done a lot in life, I never imagined being an author would be one of my accomplishments.

I had what I'd call a great childhood. My family—parents, grandparents, aunts, uncles—were always there, offering help and support whenever I needed it. They taught me the importance of leaning on one another when necessary and facing my own challenges when no one else could help. Thanks to their guidance, I learned to be patient and avoid judging until I understood the whole story. That foundation has helped me become a better husband and father.

Since elementary school, I've loved storytelling. I've always been talkative, and finally, putting my thoughts on paper with *Inconceivable Truths* has been incredibly rewarding. My writing style is conversational, like sitting with family or friends, going on tangents, and weaving everything back together in the end.

Inconceivable Truths centers on one main story in my life, which made it challenging to find a clear path through it all. In my personal life, my wife and kids are truly incredible. They've supported me throughout this journey, and we're all excited to see where this adventure leads.

Thank you,

Cody

Contents

Chapter 1 – The Beginning

Life is a wild ride, and mine was no exception. It taught me early on that fairness was a fleeting illusion, and challenges were always lurking around the corner, ready to pounce when you least expected it. But one thing I've learned is that family doesn't always come in the conventional package; sometimes, they arrive when you least expect it.

I was raised by my biological mom and my adopted father, Chris, who I'll be referring to as my dad throughout my recollection of this story. While some kids had a clear picture of their biological fathers, mine remained somewhat of a mystery. He wasn't a significant part of my life, and the real father figure was Chris, who stepped in with unconditional love and care.

The story of my biological father, Kyle, began in the 90s when he met my aunt, Kari, at a bowling alley near their high school. From what I'm told, he was instantly drawn to her and made Kari feel awkward. When my mom, Kacy, confronted him about making her sister uncomfortable, she left a lasting impression on him.

Kyle couldn't shake the memory of that bold and outspoken woman, and he soon developed a deep interest in my mom. Despite the age difference, their connection was undeniable, and they started dating while they were both still in high school. Kyle was smitten, and he couldn't help but talk about her all the time to his friends.

However, beneath the surface of their love story lurked a darker side. Kyle was involved in a life of petty crime, partnering with a friend named Rick in a string of illegal activities. Stealing cars, gambling, and burglarizing houses were all part of their alleged hobbies, with Kyle as the "mastermind."

Despite Kyle's shady past, their love seemed genuine at the time. But life's storm was brewing, and soon, their lives were entangled in a web of challenges and uncertainties that put them to the test.

My mom learned about my father's crimes when Kyle's friend, James, disclosed the information to her, and the major revelation occurred when he was arrested at my mom's house. Needless to say, she was not pleased – who would be?

My mom was a woman who cared deeply about her reputation, as most people do. She had been a star athlete at her school and was well-known. Excelling in everything she tried, except basketball, which she despised due to all the running.

One night, Kyle stayed over at Rick's house along with Rick, Rick's girlfriend, Mandy, and Mandy's friend whose name I couldn't find. Mandy supposedly had her eyes set on Kyle for some time, and in the stillness of the night, when everyone was asleep, Mandy approached Kyle in the living room, and one thing led to another.

Filled with guilt, Kyle couldn't bear the weight of what he had done. He hurriedly left the house and returned home to his mom's. There, he showered, cried, and berated himself for betraying his friend and his own girlfriend by sleeping with his best friend's girl.

My mom observed a change in Kyle's behavior, and after about a week, she discovered the truth about his infidelity with Mandy. Fuming with anger and disappointment, they had a heated argument that ultimately led to their breakup.

Over the next week, my mom put Kyle through the wringer, making his life miserable from his account. This culminated in a physical altercation in the alley behind her parents' house, where she ended up kneeing him in the groin and slapping him across the face. Their relationship became a rollercoaster of constant arguments, breakups/makeups, and a lack of trust.

During one of their breaks, approximately a year later, my mom and Rick happened to cross paths at a party. My mom, drunk, and Rick, still harboring resentment toward Kyle, had a what has been described to me as an unfortunate encounter. My mom didn't share any further details of that night, possibly because she didn't want to or because her intoxication made it hard to recall. Only my mom's friend knew about her involvement with Rick, and even that remains unconfirmed.

After that party, my mom and Kyle decided to work through their issues. They had heartfelt conversations, and ultimately, my mom chose to give him another chance, and they were able to reconcile. Around two months after getting back together, my mom discovered she was pregnant with me, and she was just nineteen at the time. Both of them were filled with a mix of excitement and fear as they prepared to welcome a new life into the world together.

My mom wanted Kyle to step up and be responsible, just like she was trying to be. It was challenging for her to bear the weight of all the responsibilities that he should have been sharing. She invested a lot of effort into helping him become a better person, partner, and future father.

In an effort to motivate him, my mom gave Kyle an ultimatum – he had to complete his high school education if he wanted to live with her. Unfortunately, he kept betraying her trust. He would lie about attending school while engaging in shady activities like playing penny poker or stealing cars. It seemed like he might be back-sliding into his old ways, which was heartbreaking for my mom as things didn't turn out the way she was hoping. At the time of my birth, my mom was just 19 years old, and my grandparents and aunt stepped in to support her like most families would. They visited every day, helping with household chores and laundry, making sure we had food, and giving my mom much-needed company since her main companion was just me, a baby.

Despite their help, my mom made the difficult decision to stop allowing Kyle to live with her shortly after I was born. His continuous lying and ditching school, coupled with my mom's post-C-section recovery, made it clear that he wasn't ready for the responsibilities of fatherhood.

As my mom began to recover and regain mobility after a few weeks, her investigative nature emerged. She frequently caught Kyle in lies, using her car's odometer to verify his whereabouts when he claimed to be at school. His explanations didn't match the mileage, often revealing that he was either playing poker with friends or avoiding his responsibilities altogether. This pattern of behavior continued for about two weeks, leading my mom to realize that he was not only neglecting her but also abandoning his role as a father, which she found unforgivable. Putting two and two together, my mom knew she had to move on and end the relationship.

Thus, when I was one month old, they decided to part ways again, once and for all.

After about a year of split, my biological father, Kyle, got caught by the police and sentenced to prison for 12 years. During this time, my mom met the man who would eventually become my dad.

During the first year of his imprisonment, Kyle would send letters to my mom and me, primarily on major holidays, but gradually, the frequency reduced to about once a month. As I grew older and read through a few of his letters, I couldn't help but cringe at the numerous grammatical mistakes and lack of proper punctuation and spelling. It was evident that his decision to ditch school and engage in illegal activities had left him ill-equipped academically.

On the other hand, my adoptive father, Chris, took a different path after high school. He enlisted in the Marines as a helicopter mechanic, serving for six years. During his time at tech school in NAS Millington, he met his first wife, Kelly, who gave him his first non-biological child, my step-sister Jessica. Unfortunately, their marriage faced challenges when she cheated on him during his deployments, ultimately leading to their divorce.

My dad was the oldest of three brothers. One of his brothers became a Deputy Sheriff in Nevada, while the youngest brother owns a Graphic Design Studio in Nevada. Chris himself went on to establish a small HVAC company. He was born in California but grew up in Arizona with his mom, who was originally from

Oklahoma. However, he still doesn't speak much about his background or upbringing. When Chris first crossed paths with my mom in 1992, he was 24 years old, and she was 20. They met at a daytime wedding. Despite feeling like he hadn't gathered enough 'liquid courage' yet, Chris was captivated by my mom's beauty as he saw her heading toward the exit after the ceremony. Buzzed and unsure of how to approach her, he enlisted the help of his youngest brother to get her number. His brother went up to my mom and managed to get her number for him, kicking off the beginning of their love story.

After a day or two of waiting, Chris mustered the courage to call and ask my mom out on a date. They decided to have brunch at a vegan restaurant, which was a refreshing change for her after enduring a destructive and toxic relationship with my biological father, Kyle. To avoid scaring Chris away on their first date, my mom chose not to reveal my identity just yet. She wanted to get to know him better and have a few more dates before disclosing the fact that she had a newborn son.

During their brunch conversation, my mom playfully teased Chris for not having the guts to approach her directly. To get to know him better, she asked about his birthday, not anticipating that her own revelation was just around the corner. Chris responded that his birthday was on February 13th.

This coincidentally happened to be the same day as my own birthday, which my mom couldn't resist mentioning.

Her confession surprised Chris, and my mom worried that it might end their relationship before it could ever start. However, he remained calm and asked questions about me. Learning that she was a mom, Chris asked about my age. My mom, feeling a bit unsure, revealed that I was six months old. Despite the unexpected news, the date went well.

After the brunch, Chris dropped my mom off at home, and they continued to go on more dates. Eventually, he asked her if she wanted to bring me along, given my mom had told him I was a really well-behaved baby. However, on the day of that crucial date, things took an unexpected turn—I was crying and screaming, completely embarrassing my mom in front of him and all the other customers at the restaurant. But Chris took it in stride, laughing and showing his willingness to stay and help.

From that point on, I have been told many stories of going out with my mom and dad.

The years passed swiftly, and throughout all their ups and downs, Chris remained a constant in my life. He continued to be there for me in every way, picking me up from school, attending all my events, and offering support whenever I needed it.

Right from the beginning, I knew that Chris was not my biological father. My parents were always open and honest with me, and I embraced the truth with understanding for the most part. Chris may not have been my birth father, but he was my dad in every sense of the word. His love transcended any blood connection, and I felt blessed to have him as a guiding force in my life.

As my mom and Chris's relationship blossomed, they moved in together after dating for a year or two. Their love story culminated in a joyful and planned wedding in Vegas, surrounded by close friends and family. I was only six at the time, and little did I know that this happy marriage would endure for 25 years and counting.

Two years into their marriage, I had the emotional experience of being officially adopted by Chris. The day is etched in my memory as if it happened just yesterday. Sitting in front of the judge alongside my mom and Chris, my heart was filled with love and excitement. My mom, with her eyes filled with pride, told me that I could change my name to any name I desired.

As an eight-year-old, the prospect of choosing my own name was both exciting and intimidating. But my love for Chris was so profound that I yearned to be a part of him in every way possible. With tears in his eyes, he listened as I requested to be named 'Christopher Gilmore the Second' after him. However, my mom laughed affectionately, and my request to take on his full name as a junior was met with gentle refusal. Nonetheless, my name ended up as Cody Gilmore, but it didn't change the profound impact of this beautiful moment. I truly do tear up just thinking about that day.

The adoption holds immense significance to me beyond mere legalities. It symbolizes the boundless love and commitment Chris has shown me as his adoptive son. His sacrifices and dedication have paved the way for the opportunities and support I have received throughout my life. In my eyes, he is the greatest man, a true father who raised me with unconditional love and care.

The love and admiration I feel for my dad are beyond words. I remain in awe of the man he is and the profound impact he has had on shaping the person I am today. I am forever grateful for his love, guidance, and presence in my life. I eagerly look forward to the continued journey with him as my rock. This chapter may have come to a close, but the story of our family's love and strength is just beginning.

Chapter 2 – Imprisoned

My journey to becoming the person I am today wasn't without its challenges, though it may seem so from the outside looking in. Life is unpredictable, and we can't always control the situations that come our way; acknowledging this truth is essential.

My dad played a crucial role in shaping the person I am. He cared for me as if I were his own son, and I couldn't have asked for a better father figure. The adoption process, which occurred when I was eight years old, wasn't a simple one. It was made possible because my biological father willingly renounced his parental rights over me. This allowed Chris to initiate the adoption process with the support of my mom and me. However, my biological father had to face the consequences of his past actions.

My biological father's life had been marked by criminal activities and run-ins with the law. He had been sentenced to 12 years in prison for various offenses, including check forgery, burglary, and theft. Despite his involvement in multiple criminal activities, he managed to evade arrest for a bit, making him seem relatively lucky. However, his luck ran out when he attempted to forge a check for around $ 5,000 at a bank.

Not thinking of the red flags he would attract with such a large amount at such a young age, he aroused suspicion from the bank staff. The security cameras were activated, the manager was alerted, and ultimately, the police were notified. His poorly planned attempt at check forgery led to his arrest. Despite being sentenced to 7 - 12 years, he ended up serving the full 12-year sentence.

My grandparents were calmly watching TV when they heard a knock on the door. My grandpa called out to my Aunt Kari to answer the door. To her surprise, it was the police at the door.

"Uhm, you want to come to the door? The cops are here," she informed my grandparents.

My grandpa took the lead, inviting the officers inside. They explained that they were looking for a Mr. Kyle Nelson and inquired if my grandparents knew his whereabouts.

"Come on in, I'll call him out for you," my grandpa said, not hiding his lack of fondness for Kyle and his willingness to cooperate with the police.

As Kyle came around the corner of the hallway, he realized the situation he was in. The officers wasted no time in placing handcuffs on him, stating that he was being taken to the station for check forgery. Kyle knew he was in trouble and regretted his actions.

The officers thanked my grandpa for his cooperation, and he replied, "Anytime, Officer." With that, they led Kyle out of the front door, and my grandparents were left to process the unexpected turn of events.

This incident was just one chapter in the complex story of my family's life, and it served as a reminder of the consequences of one's actions. While my grandparents dealt with the situation calmly, it was undoubtedly a moment that left a lasting impression on them and the family as a whole.

A few months later, my mom received a letter from Kyle while he was in prison. The letter contained a passage that was taken as threatening and unsettling, expressing his desire to be involved in my life as a father. My mom, understandably worried about the implications of the letter, sought guidance from my grandparents and family friends who held significant influence in the city's legal and judicial system.

Drawing upon their connections and favors, my mom took decisive action to ensure her and my safety and well-being. She worked tirelessly to secure full custody of me, knowing that it was crucial to keep Kyle away from my life. My family's efforts to protect me were unwavering, and they went to great lengths to keep Kyle at a distance. The consequences of his actions landed him in the isolation of solitary confinement for 30-day stretches, which took a toll on him emotionally and mentally.

While I do not know the full extent of the hardships he endured in prison, I have heard from him that his ultimate desire was to have a chance to be a father in my life and be with my mother. However, my mom believes there were other motivations behind his actions that he might not have revealed to me.

As I reflect on this portion of my life, I recognize that both parties have their own perspectives and truths regarding the situation. While my mom's actions were driven by the need to protect me, Kyle's intentions and emotions may have been more complex. I do not feel the need to delve too deeply into the details or uncover absolute truths, as people's memories and perspectives can change as they age. I'll never know exactly what was charging their decisions or actions, and I have made peace with that.

For me, what's essential is that my family and mom ensure my safety and surround me with love and support. The experience helped shape the person I am today, and I am grateful for the protective shield they provided during those challenging times. As the years passed, it became clear that Kyle and my family would never see eye-to-eye on the matter, and I've come to accept that some things may never find resolution.

My mom and grandparents were always kind and compassionate individuals who wouldn't resort to committing any harmful acts against my biological father. They were not the type to seek revenge or inflict additional suffering on others. Despite the threatening letter my mom received, she didn't use any of her connections to push for a harsher sentence or treatment for him while he was in custody. She didn't want to add more pain to his life, showing a level of generosity and compassion even in difficult circumstances.

In fact, my mom had shown remarkable restraint and understanding, as she never even disclosed to her parents that my biological father had cheated on her. She chose not to create unnecessary trouble or spread negative emotions, opting instead to handle the situation with discretion and grace.

While the relationship between my mom and my biological father was complicated, it is evident that my mom chose to take the high road and handle the situation with empathy. Her actions reflect her strong character and the value she places on showing kindness even when faced with adversity.

As time passed, my family's approach to the situation and their decision to protect me ultimately helped shape a healthier and happier environment for my upbringing. It taught me the importance of forgiveness, empathy, and the strength that comes from choosing to act with compassion, even in challenging circumstances.

Though my early life was not without its fair share of challenges and complexities, the love and care I received from Chris and my family played a significant role in shaping my life and helping me become the person I am today.

Chapter 3 – Childhood

My early childhood with my mom and dad was, by all accounts, amazing. They showered me with love and acceptance, making me feel like I truly belonged. Their watchful eyes ensured I was well taken care of, but life had other plans, and challenges soon came my way.

At the tender age of four, I was diagnosed with Panayiotopoulos Syndrome, a specific form of epilepsy more common in children. Unlike typical seizures, mine could last up to two days, which brought immense hardships.

I vividly recall one particularly tough episode when I threw up 27 times in a single day, rushing to the nearest bathroom almost every 45-50 minutes. It was a distressing experience, prompting my doctors to prescribe aggressive medication. At just seven years old, I found myself taking nine pills daily—an almost unbearable burden for a child my age. Yet, during it all, I couldn't help but compare my struggles to the children facing even more invasive treatments. This perspective helped me see myself as one of the luckier ones, or so my parents and I convinced ourselves.

The medication took its toll, causing me to become lethargic and gain weight by the time I turned eight. I transformed into a "husky," unmotivated kid, burying any inclination to be athletic or active. My self-esteem suffered a severe blow at a young age, and it seemed like an insurmountable obstacle. However, as I entered puberty, things improved significantly, granting me the years of reprieve my doctors told me would come.

Throughout my childhood, my mom and dad made sure to create memorable experiences for us. Summer months were filled with road trips and vacations, one of the most memorable being when we traveled to Memphis, Tennessee, to celebrate his daughter Jessica's high school graduation with her mom's side of the family. We also spent our time by the lakes and rivers near our home, where we'd take the boat out to wakeboard, tube, and attempt to water ski—activities I loved.

One unique quirk my dad had was an intense fear of sharks, likely stemming from an early encounter with the movie, 'Jaws.' Despite this fear, he paradoxically loved being in the water, which made our family cruises a bit amusing. On these cruises, such as the ones to the Mexican Riviera and the Disney Cruise, he usually stayed on the ship, occasionally joining my mom and me for an excursion on a dinghy.

My dad had been married once before, and he had adopted Jessica, his former wife's daughter, just as he had adopted me. Unfortunately, his first marriage ended due to his wife's infidelity, leaving him with deep emotional scars. Even though he wanted to maintain a relationship with Jessica, her mom restricted their contact, causing my dad immense pain. During my adulthood, he would occasionally open up about these emotions, knowing that one day I would better understand his struggles and heartache.

Life was a mix of challenges and cherished moments, and my family played an integral role in shaping the person I have become. Little did I know that the experiences of my youth would pave the way for a deeper understanding of life's complexities as I matured.

At a young age, I had already encountered numerous troubles and tragedies, which instilled in me the resilience and adaptability that I carry with me to this day. Challenges and diversity are something I crave, thanks to the robust foundation I had built throughout those early experiences. My family's roots ran deep in the same city for five generations, and I followed suit by attending the same schools my mom and aunt had attended. Growing up in the neighborhood where my mom spent her childhood was a nostalgic connection I cherished.

Sharing teachers with my mom, who had attended the same schools, filled me with a sense of pride. It felt like a unique bond; I considered it the coolest thing in the world. I developed close friendships in the neighborhood with Jr, Cameron, Martin, and James, who remained my best friends from elementary to early high school. Together, we navigated our school years and sports, creating an unbreakable bond.

Sports, particularly baseball, captured my heart early, and my friends shared the same passion. We spent endless hours playing on the baseball field, whether it was after school, on weekends, or at practice. With Jr at second, Cam and Martin on Shortstop and 1st Base, respectively, James at third, and me behind the plate, we formed a well-coordinated team, honing our skills year after year. We were like a well-oiled machine, and as we grew older, we welcomed new players into the outfield, maintaining our strong camaraderie.

Weekends were filled with sleepovers at each other's houses, rotating between Cam's, Jr's, and mine, though I don't recall ever staying overnight at Martin's. Our childhood was full of joy and laughter; despite any challenges we faced individually, everything felt right when we were together. We were lucky to have received wholesome upbringings and held unwavering trust in our parents. They were always there for us, ready to listen and support us through any difficulty, and they taught us valuable life lessons that shaped us into responsible individuals.

However, as we approached our teenage years, the demands of school and sports began to create a distance between us. Our once inseparable bond started to fade as we juggled our hectic schedules. Nevertheless, the memories of our carefree childhood remained etched in our hearts, reminding us of the strong foundation we had built together.

As life moved forward, we learned that it wasn't always smooth sailing, and we had to face the reality that challenges and changes were a part of growing up. As we got involved in various non-academic activities, we began to drift apart, and the distance in our friendship became more apparent. My interest in music, particularly drumming, blossomed during middle school, becoming a significant passion alongside my love for baseball. My parents supported my musical aspirations and enrolled me in drumming lessons. With time and dedication, I became relatively proficient in playing the drums, and the encouragement from my family and school friends fueled my motivation to keep practicing.

In sixth grade, I joined the school band as a drummer, and by seventh grade, I had earned the first chair percussion position for the following two years—an achievement I was immensely proud of, considering I beat out some eighth graders.

In band, I met a girl named Mari, and our friendship grew as we played on the drumline together; little did I know that friendship would last the next 15 years. I had the opportunity to explore various percussion instruments like the Snare drum, Drum set, Timpani, Bass Drum, and Xylophone.

As the section leader for percussion and a teacher's aide for younger students learning to play, I had the chance to pass on my passion and knowledge to others. I spent two years working with my band leader, assisting and guiding younger kids and helping them develop their creative skills.

My dedication to music led me to audition for the jazz academy, and to my delight, I got selected. This opened doors to numerous opportunities, and I found myself playing at concerts, different shows, venues, street fairs, and jazz competitions—all of which were incredible.

My short-lived music career was an immensely satisfying experience. The joy of performing with a group after months of practice and witnessing a flawless performance from the stage was indescribable. It taught me the beauty of collaboration, dedication, and the power of music to bring people together. Those moments on stage were nothing short of magical, filling my heart with a sense of fulfillment and contentment.

As I delved into the world of music, I couldn't help but acknowledge that life's path was taking me on a different journey, one that diverged from the tight-knit camaraderie of my childhood friendships. Nevertheless, I knew that the memories and bonds we had formed would forever hold a special place in my heart. And though we may have drifted apart, the experiences we shared remained a cherished part of my journey.

***

As life progressed, I stumbled upon Amanda practicing volleyball on the basketball court after school. Her skill and love for the sport captivated me, and I found myself eager to learn more about it. Intrigued, I asked to join her in playing, and she graciously agreed to teach me the fundamentals of volleyball. As I practiced with her, I became enamored with the sport, and little did I know, this encounter would shape my future in unforeseen ways.

With my newfound passion for volleyball, I saw an opportunity to pursue sports scholarships, which motivated me to keep going. As a bonus, I had stopped taking medications from my childhood, and my physical improvements were visible—I had lost weight and felt more agile and energetic than ever before. My friendship with Amanda proved beneficial as we practiced together frequently, pushing each other to improve. A turning point came when Amanda referred me to a woman who had run major volleyball camps in the Southwest. She was a substitute teacher at our school and head coach of the girls' volleyball team, and she became an essential figure in my volleyball journey. With her help, I was able to join the girls' team for practice, even before entering high school. She ran hard, had fun practices, and welcomed me whenever I could go.

Volleyball soon dominated my schedule, causing my baseball practice to suffer. Despite our family's strong roots in baseball and football, I made the decision to shift my focus entirely to volleyball. It was a difficult choice, given my family's legacy in those sports, but they supported my decision. Though somewhat disappointed, they won't tell you that.

As I left baseball behind, I explored other sports like martial arts, pursuing my interest in staying physically active and busy. Achieving my Black Belt in Tang Soo Do was a significant accomplishment that took about eight years, adding to my growing list of passions and achievements.

Looking back, that chance encounter with Amanda on the basketball court changed the course of my life. Volleyball became my primary pursuit, and little did I know that this sport would open doors to unforeseen opportunities and become an integral part of my identity and future endeavors. While it may have initially surprised and even disappointed some in my family, their unwavering support eventually eased their hearts, knowing I was following my true passion. My journey in volleyball was beginning, and I was eager to embrace the possibilities that lay ahead.

I rarely regret any decision I make for myself, and investing my time in other sports was one of them. When I got involved in other sports activities, I met two people, George and Zach, who would then become my best friends.

One night, all four of us were together, and it sticks out in my memory. It was in the middle of summer, and George and I got invited to a house party down the road from my house on the east side. We knew we were going to go since there would be free liquor, spades, and dominoes—our kind of scene.

So, around lunchtime, we picked up Mari and went to The Taco Shop nearby. As we sat there, we talked about the people we would see at the party, most of whom we hadn't seen since the last school year. Just then, Zach called. Without hesitation, I invited him to join us at the party. Luckily, Mari was there to help me convince his mom that it would be "safe." All I had to do was ensure we got him home safely, and we did just that, although the time in between was a bit of a shitshow.

At the party, George and I had a great time playing spades and drinking games. We were so caught up in our fun that we completely left Zach to his own devices and Mari, who we assumed was working the room as her normal self, the social butterfly.

Suddenly, a group of three guys entered the house, and our attention was drawn to the door. George saw them look at the guy who was passed out on the couch, and then he saw them look at each other and then back at the couch. He said quietly, "We gotta go." I was dismissive at first, asking why. But then, a bottle broke over the sleeping guy's head, and I quickly understood why we needed to leave.

"Hey, Mari?!?" George shouted.

"Mari?!?" I followed.

"What?" a squeaky voice said from outside.

Luckily, Mari was outside with her friends, who were smoking, and she hadn't seen what happened inside. We told her we needed to leave and started jogging quickly to the car down the block. Suddenly, we heard the sound of gunshots.

"Shots! Get to the fucking car!" I yelled.

...

"FUCK, WHERE'S ZACH?!?" George and I were pale, standing behind the car.

"We gotta go get him!"

...

...

"Guys, I am right here; let's fucking go!!!!" Zach said from the backseat, hitting the headrest of the car.

George and I burst into laughter, relieved that Zach was safe. We got in the car and drove to IHOP, our usual spot after one of our crazy nights, to wrap up and decompress from the chaotic events we had just experienced.

Throughout high school, we were inseparable—George, Mari, and I. We did everything together, from going to parties that got way out of control to spending hours at Main Street Pool Hall, trying to hustle a couple of dollars out of anyone willing to play.

Today, George and I still meet monthly, usually for a round of golf. We catch up on all the bullshit of our daily mundane lives and reminisce about the times when we thought we were 'badasses.' He is now married to a great woman and has a beautiful daughter whom he has adopted. As for Zach, he remains one of my oldest friends, and even though our busy lives sometimes keep us apart, our friendship remains as strong as ever.

***

As time went on, I found myself embracing a fighting persona in real life, behaving somewhat like an antagonist. It became almost like a "career" for me as I engaged in fights with a few people at parties and during kickbacks. Surprisingly, my friends didn't view me as someone with anger issues; they accepted this aggressive side of me alongside the playful joker I had always been.

Humor was and is a big part of my personality, and I often used it to diffuse conflicts and turn tense situations into jokes. However, not everyone in my circle appreciated this style of humor. Some couldn't handle the jokes, while others lacked the wit to come back with something funny, which led them to perceive me as an asshole, which admittedly sometimes I was. There were instances when I didn't realize when the joke crossed the line and came off as mean. But for me, joking around and teasing were ways to bond with the people I cared about and respected.

I had a rule of only joking with those I loved and admired. For me, it was a way of expressing affection and camaraderie. If someone couldn't handle a joke or some light ribbing from time to time, I didn't see them as particularly fun or someone I'd enjoy spending time with. I valued the ability to share a good laugh and not take things too seriously, as it brought joy and a sense of connection among friends.

Despite my aggressive streak and sometimes coming off as an asshole, I remained true to myself and maintained the friendships that mattered most.

My friends understood my intentions, and I continued to be the joker and fighter, unapologetically expressing my genuine self to those I held close.

Chapter 4 – School Days

When I turned 12, my mom and I discussed reaching out to my biological father, Kyle. After that day, the idea was constantly on my mind. Despite all the crazy things I've done and my mom's affectionate nature, I still had this strong desire to meet Kyle. I struggled for a long time, battling my thoughts and feeling uncomfortable about how my mom would react to such a monumental decision. So, we decided to wait until I was older and mentally prepared.

By the time I turned 16, I felt I needed to meet the person I came from. It felt strange to go straight to my mom and talk about wanting to meet my biological father. Despite my discomfort, I gathered my courage and had a conversation with her. To my surprise, she listened and allowed me to talk to Kyle.

I wasn't expecting her to say "okay," knowing it must have been hard for her. She arranged a meeting with Kyle within two weeks but cautioned me about his personality and fake emotions. She warned me, "You don't know Kyle the way we do. He's always been a liar, good at fooling people."

Chris, my dad, also shared his concerns with a warning voice. He didn't want me to get manipulated or misled by Kyle. He said, "He's likable but manipulative. Don't let him lead you into anything that will leave you believing his lies. Stay aware, no matter what he says."

I appreciated their honesty and concern as I prepared to meet my biological father.

"Okay, I understand; I'll be cautious," I assured them. "I've called him and asked him to meet you at the mall down the street," she confirmed, but I could sense the fear she was feeling. "And one more thing, you'll be sitting at a table with him, but don't worry. We'll be sitting right behind you so you can see us. Feel free to talk to him openly," Chris said, fulfilling his responsibility as a protective father. "I... I feel bad that you both have been so worried about this; I still want to meet my biological father," I said hesitantly. "You don't need to feel bad. It's your right to meet the person you came from," she comforted me, patting me on the back.

***

We went down to the street and sat in the way we had discussed. After a few minutes, Kyle joined us. It was my first time seeing him, and I wasn't sure why I wanted to interact with him. My first impression of him wasn't particularly impressive; he didn't have a remarkable size or stature. His shaved head and tiny mustache made me judge immediately. As I tried to find some similarity with him, I realized that I only resembled my mom.

He stood about a foot away from me and seemed quite nervous. I sensed that he wanted to hug me, but I stayed still. Although he smiled throughout the meeting, his hands were shaking, and he sounded kind of like a hippie.

He sat across from me and tried to start a conversation with some unnecessary questions for about 30 minutes.

"Hey, Cody. How have you been?" Kyle asked, his voice filled with gratitude.

"He... Hey... I'm good," I hesitated because the person sitting right beside me was my biological father, who hadn't been a part of my life until I reached out to meet him.

"I know anyone's life can't be good without their father," Kyle said, looking down, and I couldn't quite figure out if he was genuinely ashamed or just pretending.

Early on, my mom taught me to be a keen observer and look into things further than surface level. I didn't find Kyle to be an empathetic person, so I decided to challenge him with multiple strange questions to see if his two-faced personality would reveal itself.

"Uhm, so how long were you in prison?" I asked, throwing a bold question at my father.

"We should talk about something else. Don't you think so?" Kyle tried to divert the conversation.

"What's your favorite color?" I continued with annoying questions.

"Where is this coming from?" he replied, clearly annoyed.

Inside, I was disappointed that I hadn't missed anything, especially not having a "real" dad. After that first interaction, I decided I didn't need this guy in my life and that I would do my best to avoid becoming like him. Fortunately, Chris, my dad, was already fulfilling the role of a loving and caring dad.

"So, why didn't you call me? Or did you not want to?" I asked bluntly, catching him off guard. It felt strange to do this in front of my parents, who let me ask questions freely, but I sensed their presence during the meeting. Despite that, I managed to make him uncomfortable with my questions, along with myself, which ultimately led to the meeting lasting only about 30 minutes.

The meeting wasn't very satisfying since I didn't get to know him personally, and it felt like my parents were always watching. During the encounter, I came up with a plan to get his phone number through my mom's phone, hoping to connect with him independently in the future.

"How do you feel about him?" Mom asked, wrapping her arms around her chest, awaiting an honest answer from me.

I knew my mom had always despised liars, and she used to punish me whenever I lied to her during my childhood. This time, I had to lie to spare her feelings because I wanted to have another meeting with my biological father, which wouldn't be possible if I told her the truth.

"Not really good, Mom. I didn't expect anything from his side, ya know, because he abandoned me. But I wanted to meet him to see him," I replied, turning my face away. I didn't want her to catch my lies since she's very perceptive.

"That's what I thought. No one would like a parent who abandoned them." my mom reassured; her assumption was understandable as they both feared losing me to him for some strange reason.

Though I didn't plan to lie, I felt I had no choice. "Yeah, Mom, definitely. He's not someone I'd hang around with. It was just a meeting to see who he really is," I assured her before taking a step toward my room.

My dad stopped me, "So, are you feeling any different?"

"I didn't feel anything, really. It wasn't about emotions at all. And why would I need someone like him when I already have a dad?" I gave him a hug and thought, at least that one isn't a lie.

He embraced me tightly, and I hugged him back to offer comfort. They seemed relieved to hear my opinion, but I couldn't shake their curiosity about meeting Kyle again.

Despite telling my parents that I didn't care about Kyle, the truth was that I intended to meet him alone because I wanted to learn everything about him. I hoped that by doing so, I could avoid making the same mistakes he did.

***

A couple of months had passed since my last meeting with Kyle, so I decided to text him for another meeting.

"Hey Kyle, I hope you're doin' good. Our first meeting didn't go as I wanted, so I'd like to meet again if you're up for it. Let me know if you're free. - Cody."

In less than five minutes, I received his reply: "Cody, It's great to hear from you, and I appreciate you reaching out. I'm looking forward to seeing you. I'm having a BBQ at my place on Sunday, and I'd love for you to come. Kyle."

To ensure there were no hiccups, I decided to tell my best friend, George, about my plan with Kyle.

Everyone in the house was asleep, so I called George with a hushed tone.

"Oh hey... hey, dude. It's 3 A.M.....WHY?" George answered with a sleepy voice.

"I need to ask you something; wake up!" I whispered.

"You good?" George asked with concern.

"I just texted Kyle and asked him to meet up, and he said he could on Sunday," I replied, aware that my parents could wake up any minute.

"What? Why?" George inquired.

"I really want to meet him. He's not someone I'd ever want to hang out with, but I still want to talk to him on my own terms. At the first meeting, my parents were watching everything, and I couldn't really understand him. I want to know more about him, his family, and his... his daughter, my half-sister," I explained.

"But won't your mom ask where you're going? What's your plan for that?" George raised a valid concern.

"I'll tell her I'm staying at your place for the weekend after school, and I'll be back Sunday night," I said.

"I'm down, but are you sure, man? It's risky. Your mom will kill both of us if she finds out," George tried to dissuade me, but I had already made up my mind.

"George, I've planned everything. You tell the same thing to your mom, and then we will go to the BBQ," I declared.

*****

The next morning, George and I took off and headed to the north side of town, which was about 45 minutes away from where he lived. It started raining on the way, but we followed the directions and eventually reached my Kyles' house. When we stepped inside, he was watching football. His family room was like a football field adorned with Redskins memorabilia. I learned that day that he was a huge fan of the Washington Redskins. We were warmly welcomed by everyone there, and George and I spent the whole day talking, laughing, and having fun.

As the day went on, I realized that my initial judgment of him may have been too hasty. He seemed like a different person than I had expected. Soon, an older woman came into the room, and Kyle introduced her as his mom. I greeted her respectfully, although I was puzzled because I had never met her before, and she seemed to know me. As we continued talking, Kyle's sister also entered the room, and I was introduced to her as well. We all had a great time together, and I also got to meet my half-sister, Hannah, who is a few years younger than me.

At one point, Kyle asked if I would like to step outside for a bit of privacy, and I agreed. Once outside, I decided to ask him about his time in prison.

"So, what was it like being in prison for such a long time?" I inquired, wanting to understand more about his past.

He looked and sounded sorrowful as he replied, "Well, I don't think I need to say it was horrible. Prison is not a place where anyone would want to spend any amount of time. It felt like being on autopilot where you don't have to do anything; you just let it keep going. Those years sucked, buddy."

His response gave me a glimpse of the hardships he had faced during those years, and it made me feel a mix of emotions toward him.

"Speaking the truth, I can't undo what's happened. I still can't believe some of the most important years of my life were spent in prison," Kyle said, wiping his tears with a napkin.

"It sounds terrible to even hear about it. I can't imagine how you got through that for all those years," I sighed, extending my hand as a gesture of support.

At that moment, Kyle felt like the most stupid person on Earth for talking about his imprisonment experience. He wondered why I had even brought it up. "I actually ended up in prison for check fraud. It might be hard for you to believe. Can you believe someone walks into a bank to cash a $5000 check and BOOM. Arrested!" He let out a humorless laugh while patting my back.

Later that night, Kyle was treated to a barbecue at his place. Every passing moment of that memorable night revealed a fun-loving, crazy guy who wanted to savor every bit of life. George and I had an amazing time there, and we didn't want the night to end. At some point during the party, Rick, Kyle's best friend, arrived with his wife and daughters, one of whom was named Paige.

At first glance, Paige caught my eye, and I couldn't help but think, "Beautiful." Rick introduced himself and extended his hand for a handshake, mentioning that Kyle had talked about me.

"Nice to meet you," I replied while sneaking glances at Paige, captivated by her appealing personality. I was more interested in talking to her than engaging in a conversation with Rick.

Rick smirked and said, "Kyle talks about you a lot, and it seems like it's all true."

Inside, I felt a twinge of remorse for sneaking out and lying to my parents. I knew my actions were unjustifiable, but I believed I had the right to meet my father and get to know him. Despite my dad and mom providing me with the best upbringing, lying around them was never something I enjoyed. Circumstances led me to do so, but at that moment, I felt it was worth it. I got to know my biological father and also met a beautiful girl.

Chapter 5 – Dating

Life is pretty strange, especially when you're a young adult still figuring things out. Through everything, love is often the solace we seek. I've had my fair share of love - dating, falling hard, and dealing with heartbreak, but I wouldn't change a thing about it.

Like everyone else, my dating life has played a significant role in shaping me, even though it may not be as thrilling as some epic tale. Funny enough, when I first met Paige, we didn't even talk. It's a little lie, I tell myself, alongside all the other secrets I keep locked away.

It started when I was a sophomore in high school and began dating my long-time high school girlfriend, Anastasia. We made it work despite attending different schools in different cities. Both of us were athletes, and we'd support each other by going to each other's sporting events or meeting up over the weekends. This went on for four years off and on, but eventually, we decided to end things for good around when I started college.

It was around the time I met Paige at a BBQ party hosted by Kyle. She was with her dad, Rick, who happened to be Kyle's best friend. I couldn't help but notice how pretty she was, and I mentioned it to George.

"Wow, she's pretty. I'm gonna go talk to her," I said, eager to strike up a conversation.

George warned me, "Alright, man, do your thing."

But I approached her anyway, and we hit it off. I asked for her number, and we started texting and talking regularly. Eventually, we went out with some friends, and when she came out of her house, I couldn't help but be captivated by her all over again.

I have to admit, as a healthy young guy, I had my desires and appreciated the good things life had to offer. As we drove off, I can't recall exactly where we went that first night. It might have been a café, or perhaps we caught a movie, or maybe it was a combination of both. The details are hazy, but what I do remember is the conversation we had while enjoying our food.

She asked me, "So, what are you looking for?"

I wasn't one to beat around the bush, so I replied honestly, "I'm not looking for a serious relationship. I like you, and I think you're cool. We could hang out as friends and see where things go, you know, if there's a spark."

Paige smiled and said, "So, like a friends-with-benefits situation?"

"That'd be great! We could be FWBs. If you're cool with that?"

She chuckled, nodded, and said, "Alright, we could give it a try. I'm not looking for anything serious either at the moment."

I wanted to make sure she wasn't just agreeing because I wanted a FWB arrangement, so I asked, "Are you sure you're not doing this just to go along with it?"

Confused, she asked, "What do you mean?"

I explained, "I'm a pretty straightforward guy. I don't like leading people on or playing with their feelings too much. Girls often go along with things they don't really want to avoid problems or hurting the dude's feelings. I don't want that to happen here."

Paige reassured me, "Oh, I understand. I appreciate that you're honest and straightforward. Most guys out there lie to get in a girl's pants, but meeting someone like you is different. At least you're honest about what you want."

"Okay then, we're on the same page. Good," I said, relieved.

After that open conversation, we wrapped up our little "date," and I dropped her off at her house. It turned out to be the first and last official date we had, but we continued hanging out a lot, especially at the parties I threw at my place. She became part of my close circle of friends, and over time, our relationship evolved into something physical. We met up regularly, and this arrangement worked smoothly for a year or so without any major issues.

One day, I went to pick up Paige from her house to go somewhere with George and me. As I parked my car by the curb and was about to text her to come out, her father, Rick, approached my car window. He told me, "This isn't a fast-food drive-through. You have to come to the door to pick up my daughter."

"Sure, no problem. Won't happen again," I replied.

Feeling a bit uneasy, I entered their house with George following me. We sat down and waited for Paige as she was still getting ready. Inside, Rick introduced himself and his wife, Karen, in a formal manner. Everything seemed normal, but things took an unexpected turn when Karen went into the kitchen to get drinks.

Rick leaned in and whispered in my ear, "You know, I had your mom, too, in high school."

I was taken aback by what he said. In my head, I thought, "Oh, yeah? I'm about to have your daughter."

The situation could have escalated, given that I was hot-headed. However, George sensed the tension and quickly pulled me out of the house. We waited in the car, and when Paige finally came out, I didn't mention what Rick had said to me. I also kept this from my mom; it was just too awkward and uncomfortable to talk about her sexual history, and it was definitely not on my list of things to do.

After the altercations with Rick, I probably should have ended things with Paige, but I couldn't bring myself to do it. I also didn't tell my parents who she really was, although I did introduce Paige to them once at a party. I used to throw parties at my house regularly, and admittedly, some of those were partly to see Paige. However, because of the way my mom raised me, I felt obligated to introduce her to my parents.

For several reasons, I decided not to reveal Paige's last name during the introduction. Firstly, I wasn't sure if what Rick said about my mom was true, and I didn't want to open up on that potentially sensitive topic. If Rick's claim about my mom were true, it would undoubtedly make my mom feel uncomfortable, and I didn't want to put her through that awkwardness, especially if there was any truth to it.

On top of that, there was another secret I was hiding from my parents. I was still secretly meeting my biological father, Kyle, despite previously telling my parents that I wanted nothing to do with him. Revealing the truth about Paige would inevitably lead to exposing this lie as well. To avoid this complicated situation, Paige and I came up with an elaborate background story about how we had known each other for a long time, even before our official introduction. It was a wild and intricate web of lies to keep both secrets hidden.

Looking back, it was utterly insane to keep up with all these lies and half-truths. But at the time, I thought it was the best way to protect my mom and maintain a semblance of normalcy in my relationships with both her and Kyle. Little did I know that this tangled web of deception would eventually catch up to me.

Anyway, we had this fling going on for about a year – she would come to my house, or I'd pick her up, and we'd drive around to find a safe and secluded spot to fool around. One time, we parked outside a park and were fooling around when suddenly there was a knock on the car window. A cop was standing there, looking serious, and I thought we were in trouble for public indecency, which was/is a big deal.

We somehow dealt with the cop and quickly drove away. Around the same time, we found a perfect spot behind a hotel that was very secluded from, well, almost anybody. So, we used that spot many times.

It wasn't always just about physical intimacy, though. We'd sit in the car and talk about life and everything in between. Being around her was fun, and I felt comfortable in her presence. That's why the arrangement continued even after she moved out of Rick's place and got her own apartment.

However, good things do have an expiration date. Our arrangement came to an end when I told her I wanted to ask out another girl I was interested in, but I suggested we could still continue our thing if it didn't work out with the new girl. She wasn't happy with this and said she didn't want to be second best again. So, we agreed to stop entirely and resume only if both of us were single and willing to restart the arrangement.

When I told Paige about the girl I was interested in dating (to see what it was like and if there was potential for more), I suggested we could slow things down between us instead of ending it completely. She replied that, again, she didn't want to be a second option, so she thought it was best to stop. I have a policy that, even in casual hookups, I don't switch partners once we're getting close to exclusivity. So, when we had our arrangement, I was only with her physically. But with dating, it was different. I couldn't date one person and sleep around with another.

We ended things amicably, and I reiterated that I was just a text away if she ever wanted to resume the arrangement (assuming I was single at that time), and she agreed. We parted ways on good terms because we had been honest from the beginning about what we wanted.

So, we stopped seeing each other. It was as simple as that! I asked out the girl I was interested in, and we started dating, but it didn't turn out as I expected. After dating for about three or four months, I didn't see it going anywhere serious or better, so we broke up and went our separate ways.

Now, when it comes to the interesting part, I wasn't too heartbroken about the breakup because I expected Paige to be there, and we'd pick up where we left off. However, I didn't realize that she had moved on and was seeing someone else. When I approached her after becoming single again, she was in a relationship with another guy.

I tried my best to convince her to cheat on her boyfriend and be with me as well, but she didn't budge. As a result, I redirected my feelings toward other women and leaned into promiscuity. I dated many women, but my interactions with them were mostly focused on the physical, which earned me a reputation as a player, but I was fine with that label at the time.

Unknowingly, I was trying to suppress my true feelings for Paige and Anastasia by engaging in these behaviors. I was successful in keeping my emotions buried until the end of that year when Paige texted me that she had broken up with her boyfriend and was single again. She asked if I was seeing anyone, and I said no. Technically, I wasn't in a committed relationship, but I was involved with multiple women.

I was both excited and anxious when she texted me out of the blue, hinting at the possibility of rekindling our connection. I had strong feelings for her, and I knew she felt the same way. However, I wasn't ready to face the reality of the situation.

So, we decided to get back together and continue our casual relationship, which went well for a few months until a serious conversation came up. We were hanging out at her apartment when Paige finally brought up the topic we had been avoiding. Paige tried to have "THAT" conversation with me, but I kept avoiding it, not wanting this honeymoon period to end.

Then, she revealed her decision to join the Air Force, which caught me by surprise. I didn't know how to respond initially, just saying, "For real?" But when she asked if we should talk about getting serious, I evaded the question and only wanted to focus on having fun for a few more months until she was gone. This frustrated Paige, and she questioned whether I truly liked her, if the military was an issue, or if I couldn't see a future with her.

Reluctantly, I decided to be honest and told her everything. I confessed that I was concerned about how my mom would react if she found out I was dating the daughter of a man she allegedly had hooked up with in high school. I knew it would devastate my mom, especially if we got married, as it would mean inviting both Rick and Kyle to the wedding. I couldn't put my mom through that, and I would always choose her over anyone else. It wasn't even a question for me.

Paige was upset when I made it clear that I would choose my mom over her, and I thought that would be the end of us forever.

Chapter 6 – Love

I wasn't a playboy, but I did play.

In fact, I never toyed with anyone's emotions, or so I thought; writing this I have realized I was kind of a piece. I communicated honestly and straightforwardly about what I wanted and was looking for, and that's how I attracted most girls. I genuinely loved women, and sometimes they loved me too! But when it came to actual love, I felt it came into my life later than I expected. I was satisfied with casual encounters and physical relationships, thinking there was no need for romantic involvement as long as my physical needs were met.

My attitude toward love and dating didn't mean I was against the idea or had never dated before. Quite the opposite, my first "real" relationship was in high school during my freshman year. The girl I dated was in the 8th grade, attending a different school in a nearby city. Since her parents were separated, she would often shuttle back and forth between cities.

At the time, I didn't have a car or a license, so I couldn't drive to her town whenever I wanted to see her. Instead, we usually met when she came to my city for the weekend, staying with her dad, who lived about two miles from my house. My parents would often drive me to her dad's house to pick her up, and then we'd spend the day together, going on dates like shopping at the mall, watching movies, eating, and having fun.

Even though I couldn't predict what the future held for us or where our relationship was heading, I was content with what we had in that present moment. Looking back, her mom and I got along really well. However, I could never quite figure out if I had won over her dad and stepdad (in hindsight, they were great at keeping everyone guessing). Similarly, my parents rooted for us and perhaps even hoped we'd be together for a long time, maybe even getting married. Although I wasn't certain about the future, I cherished whatever we had at that moment. In retrospect, we had come a long way in accepting the relationship. Initially, we didn't put labels on what we had, but as time passed, calling her "my girlfriend" became easier for me.

It was simple; we were both young, exploring ourselves and navigating the ups and downs of high school life. Both sets of parents loved having us around, so I joined them on trips and vacations along with my own family. Eventually, I got my license and a car, and that made it even easier to spend quality time together at her place or outside.

We were deeply in love and inseparable. Sometimes, we even skipped school or our practices to spend time with each other. I would drive to school, park the car in the lot, and then leave with my friends to see her. After spending time together, I would go back to school and drive my car back home.

This continued for a while, and my teammates were aware of it, but they never revealed my secret. When Anastasia got her license and a car, she did the same for me, showing that the love and affection were mutual. I even gave her a promise ring, expressing my commitment to her. I genuinely believed we would end up together, but things fell apart around the time I was starting college.

We had our fair share of ups and downs during our relationship. We had periods of not talking, but we always worked things out and got back together after talking everything out.

We both wanted the relationship to work, so it's puzzling how we ended up breaking up over a tattoo. There's some background to this: My friends George, Mari, and I had been planning to get matching tattoos of our initials, "GMC," symbolizing each of our first names. Mari and George were all set to get the tattoos, but I was still contemplating whether to get one or not. It's not that I didn't want to; I actually wanted to create this memory with my best friends.

However, Anastasia made it clear that if I got another girl's initial tattooed on my body, it would be the end of us. I was torn because I didn't want to jeopardize our relationship over a tattoo. Yet, it didn't seem fair for Anastasia to ask me to choose between my friends and her.

Despite my mom's advice, "Don't take this high school love too seriously. Your friends could be around much longer," I found myself in a difficult spot, unsure of what to do next. After receiving the advice about making sure I didn't regret my decisions, I didn't act on it until we had an argument that made me change my mind. I was determined to have the matching tattoo with my friends, and I decided to go for it despite the potential consequences.

I went ahead and got the tattoo, and when I sent Anastasia a picture of all three tattoos together, she promptly texted back that we were done. It was shocking and heartbreaking. The person I loved and saw a future with had ended our relationship because I called what I thought was a bluff.

After the breakup, I met Anastasia one last time for what turned out to be a final intimate encounter. She came to the house wearing my shirt to return some of my stuff, and we went at it one final time.

When she left without saying goodbye, I expressed that I was still open to getting back together, but she chose not to return to my life.

Looking back, I don't regret my decision, as I believe I always think things through and make logical choices. That one was less thought out, but I don't apologize for what I thought was the best choice at the time. Although I didn't expect her to end things, I had to come to terms with the fact that she was gone from my life.

In hindsight, I think she ended things to spare herself from another long-distance relationship when I was going to college. However, my plans changed due to my grandfather's illness, and we ended up in the same city again.

Two years later, we crossed paths while both were in new relationships. We had a strange conversation that felt like rekindling an old flame, even though we were trying to be friends. Talking about the breakup helped us mentally move on a bit. I knew I wouldn't cheat on my current partner, who later became the mother of my son, but I needed closure from the past relationship.

We exchanged messages for some time, but eventually, I realized that reopening that particular wound might not be a good idea. So, we decided to stop talking altogether. It wasn't too difficult, as both of us had made the decision and had to stick to it.

First love is a powerful experience that leaves a lasting mark on our memories. Every detail of the first kiss, first time holding hands, first touch, or first romantic message remains etched in our minds. It's because it's the first time we've experienced such intense feelings for someone outside our family or close friends. It might have been the moment when we truly understood that love can make life beautiful. Whatever the reasons may be, the truth is that first love is something you never forget.

Even as time goes on and we move on to happier times, the memories of first love can still make our hearts skip a beat. It's a unique and powerful emotion that remains with us forever.

Chapter 7 – Fatherhood

Becoming a father was a pleasant surprise, happening earlier than I expected. It was truly amazing, devoting myself entirely to this tiny and adorable little person, willing to sacrifice anything for them. Not all my children were planned; like Bob Ross, I affectionately call them my happy little accidents.

Let's go back to how it all started with Erica. We hadn't been seeing each other for long, just about two months when everything happened quickly and without much thought. I met Erica in 2011 at a bowling alley and was instantly drawn to her. When I asked my friend for her number, she declined, but I didn't give up. I got her number directly from her, though it cost me a relationship with that friend.

At the time, Erica was already twenty years old, a bit older than me by a year and a half. She celebrated her twenty-first birthday during pregnancy while I was still young, turning twenty, seven months before our son's birth. It felt like I was following in my mom's footsteps since she had me at nineteen.

Our parents weren't thrilled about Erica and me becoming parents at such a young age, probably recalling their own struggles. It was indeed a huge responsibility.

Despite the challenges, Erica and I got a condo where we had wonderful parties with our friends. We played games, hung out, and had a great time together.

At that time, I worked as a bouncer at a strip club, which sadly had its fair share of violence. There were fights almost every week; within my first month, there was even a shooting.

As we prepared for parenthood, our excitement grew, but so did a bit of nervousness. Erica and I may have been young, but we embraced this new responsibility with love. Little did I know, more surprises were yet to come, altering the course of our lives forever.

Obviously, Erica wasn't thrilled about my job at the strip club, but as long as it paid the bills, she didn't complain. She had quit her job due to pregnancy, which made financial matters tighter. Eventually, we moved back in with my parents, who welcomed us with open arms despite their initial reservations about the pregnancy and continued to support us even after our son was born.

Things were stable until then.

The memory of my first son's birth remains vivid in my mind. I received the call early in the morning and rushed down the street to the hospital. Erica's contractions had begun, and her water had broken.

My parents were already taking her to the hospital. The day is a bit of a blur, but it seemed like we weren't at the hospital for very long before he was there. I received the call around nine in the morning; after a few hours of labor, we held our little bundle of joy.

I was by Erica's side during her labor, and while she was enjoying the effects of the epidural, the doctor asked me to take a look as my son was crowning. It was admittedly a bit messy and intense, but my excitement to meet my son surpassed any other feelings. After a few minutes of pushing, my son was born.

As a father, you look past the blood, the pain, and the mess, and all you see is the beautiful little life in front of you. The doctor had me cut the cord and raised him up, and I was in awe, witnessing the miracle of birth. After they cleaned him up, they stamped his little feet on my white shirt using a small ink pad, a tradition my mom had advised me to be prepared for; luckily, it was still practiced at the time. This would be a cherished memory shared only with my first son, as they no longer allow it.

At that moment, I officially became a dad! Words can't fully describe the intensity of my emotions at that time. My excitement and joy reached their peak, and I felt an overwhelming sense of love for this tiny new addition to our family.

My son turned out to be a beautiful baby, weighing seven pounds and measuring nineteen and a half inches in length. I vividly remember that because he and my daughter were the same height and weight at birth. They wrapped him up and gently placed him in my arms while the medical staff tended to Erica.

Childbirth is undoubtedly an unpleasant experience, to say the least, but the aftermath is truly extraordinary. At that moment, I was a mix of emotions, both overwhelmed and emotionally drained. I looked at that little human through tear-filled eyes, experiencing a sense of wonder and love I had never known before. It was a completely unique and profound experience that heightened my emotions to a level I had never imagined.

Despite my anticipation that the newborn stage would be challenging, my son turned out to be an easy and happy baby. He hardly cried unnecessarily and didn't always demand to be held. Perhaps he was already receiving all the pampering and affection he needed, being the firstborn from both sides of the family.

Fatherhood knows no bounds. It takes on different forms and depths depending on one's perspective. I personally experienced fatherhood on three levels: the initial nervousness that comes with pregnancy, the wisdom gained as parenthood develops, and the acceptance of what my children grow into as they embrace maturity. The title of "Dad" is not simply bestowed; it must be earned.

When it came to parenting, Erica and I shared a similar mindset and set of values, reminiscent of the way people were raised in the 70s and 80s. We believed in allowing our children to explore and experience life, even if it meant facing certain challenges. Instead of imposing strict prohibitions, we preferred to guide them with honest advice, giving them the freedom to make choices and learn from the consequences.

Realism was essential in our approach to parenting. We encouraged our children to set realistic expectations and were honest with them about the challenges they might encounter. If they showed interest in something, we supported them wholeheartedly, offering guidance and reminding them that their choices were ultimately their own.

We always treated our son as a person, not just a child. We engaged him in conversations beyond baby/toddler talk, acknowledging that he would understand more as he grew older. While others might use baby talk with him, I never discouraged it, appreciating any form of kindness toward my child.

A year and a half after my son's birth, Erica and I faced some challenges in our relationship, leading me to move out and live with my grandparents temporarily. The decision was motivated by a desire to create a healthier environment for my son, away from any toxicity in our relationship. Despite the separation, I remained involved in my son's life, visiting him daily and maintaining a cordial relationship with Erica.

During this break, I met Rebecca, who would eventually become my wife. The path to happiness was not smooth and brought its share of suffering. However, in the end, it was all worth it. Erica and I have remained close, and now we are way better friends than we ever were romantic partners. We have fostered a harmonious environment for our son, ensuring he never witnesses negative talk between us about the other parent. Respect and understanding have been paramount in our co-parenting journey.

Parenthood has taught me how much parents play a pivotal role in shaping their children's worldview and character. We serve as role models, creating a nurturing and joyful atmosphere for them to grow into responsible individuals. Parenthood is a journey of continual learning, and the relationship with our children should never cease, even as they enter adulthood.

Chapter 8 – Marriage

Love at first sight is often seen as a movie cliché, but when I locked eyes with the bartender at the nightclub where I worked as a doorman, I couldn't help but believe in it. My wife was the epitome of beauty, and the sight of her left me feeling like a shy teenager with a crush all over again. I had always been confident and outgoing, but at that moment, I felt a bit overwhelmed by the intensity of my attraction to her.

As fate would have it, the club's manager, Wes, became a close friend of mine, and another bartender, who would later become the godmother to two of my children, played a pivotal role in helping me win the heart of my future wife. I was a natural gambler, and my wife would often joke that nobody should bet against me because I rarely made bets I couldn't win.

The story of how it all began involves late-night hangouts with Wes after closing down the club. We would go to his house, get drunk, and talk about everything under the sun. Music was a shared passion, so he would play the guitar while I would sing in my raspy, drunken voice. Those moments were just two buddies bonding over their shared love for music and indulging in cheap whisky.

Though our routine may not have been the healthiest, we were living in the euphoria of being carefree. The connection I felt with my future wife was undeniable, and despite her initial bet against me, I eventually won her heart. Our love story began in the magical haze of those late-night escapades, and it continues to thrive as we navigate the beautiful journey of parenthood and partnership together.

I couldn't stop talking about her, constantly bringing up my infatuation with the bartender to Wes and anyone else who would listen to me ramble. One drunk morning, tired of waiting for fate to intervene, I finally told Wes to call her. He was more than happy to help and called her right away, announcing my interest with a playful tone. She sounded a bit annoyed with him, asking if she knew me, but Wes assured her that she may not know me, but she knew who I was.

When I took the phone, I nervously introduced myself and asked if I could take her out on a date. Surprisingly, she agreed, and we quickly made plans for our first meetup. It felt like something straight out of a romantic comedy.

After a few days of late-night phone calls, we decided to meet at Wes' place and head to a country bar for some dancing. However, we soon realized that the bar was far and that the drive would take up a lot of time. Sensing my desire to get to know her better, she suggested a bar across the street from my friend's house, and I enthusiastically agreed. I was excited to have a chance to talk to her.

But then, unexpectedly, she invited Wes to join us. I looked at him, silently telling him with my eyes not to go. I wanted some privacy to get to know this woman I hoped could become my future wife. Though we all walked to the bar together, I used facial gestures to signal to Wes to come up with an excuse to leave. He found himself in a tight spot, caught between being a good friend to her and a wingman to me.

Coming in like a champion, he said he had left his wallet and ID at home, using that as an excuse to leave the bar. I appreciated his clever move, which set the stage for what would turn into one of the most unforgettable nights of my life.

As he exited the bar and didn't return, I knew it was my chance. She noticed a pool table, and it brought back memories of her childhood when she used to play with her father. Intrigued by her past, I found it fascinating since I also enjoyed playing pool, usually going to Main Street, a pool hall, with my friend George.

Excited about the prospect of playing pool with her, we played a few games. It was during these games that she finally asked me about my age, and when I revealed I was only 22, she was taken aback, exclaiming, "Holy Shit! You're just a baby, and I just turned 30."

I couldn't help but smile and retort, "Well, I'll be 23 in February."

Her laughter filled the empty barroom as she jokingly responded, "That definitely doesn't make it any better."

In hindsight, she admitted that she initially saw me as a short-term fling, perhaps a boy toy to have a few hookups with, and then part ways. But for me, there was something more profound. I felt an overwhelming connection when I was around her from the beginning, a feeling I had never experienced before. It was both perplexing and beautiful, a mix of emotions I couldn't fully comprehend.

As we continued playing pool, the rain outside started to sprinkle, creating a cozy ambiance. She lined up for the eight ball but missed the shot. It was a moment that seemed to encapsulate our budding relationship – unpredictable and full of surprises.

Little did we know that this encounter would mark the beginning of a remarkable journey together, defying age differences and expectations. I was determined to prove to her that my feelings were genuine and that I was willing to do whatever it took to make her mine.

In the end, age was just a number, and what truly mattered was the connection we shared and the love that blossomed between us. That night, playing pool and dancing in the rain, I had no idea that I was embarking on a path that would lead me to the love of my life, my soulmate, and the mom of my other three children. It was the start of a love story that would stand the test of time, and I wouldn't trade those moments for anything in the world.

As I lined up for that challenging shot on the pool table, I couldn't help but feel the pressure building. The bet was on; I had to sink the eight ball into the side pocket, and my ball was positioned about three inches to the right and an inch behind the eight ball. I saw this as an opportunity to show her that I was more mature than my age suggested. Little did I know, she was probably listening to my inner desperation as I struggled with the shot.

Then, she decided to up the stakes, making it more interesting. She proposed a bet, saying, "If you hit that eight ball into that pocket, I'll dance with you in the rain."

Curious, I asked, "Okay, and if I lose?"

"Then the date's over, and we part as friends," she replied nonchalantly, already assuming I would lose.

Realizing it was an all-or-nothing moment, I took the shot with confidence, and to my delight, the ball sank right into the pocket. She went from being dismissive to completely surprised. I revealed that I had been holding back a little, going easy on her in the first few games, and had to hustle for that victory.

Jokingly, I told her, "Going forward, you should know, never bet against me if I'm willing to take it. If I agree, I know I'm going to win. I don't gamble; I play the odds."

She soon realized she was the one who had to pay up, which she hadn't anticipated. Despite the rain having stopped a few minutes earlier, I playfully suggested she could pay me back on our second date, which she agreed to.

As we walked back to our friend Wes' house, she expressed the desire to keep talking. I noticed that park across the street from the bar and suggested we sit there for a while and continue our conversation. She happily agreed, and little did we know that this moment would mark the beginning of something special. That night, under the dim streetlights in the park, we talked and laughed, connecting on a level that went beyond age and expectations. It was the start of a beautiful journey that would lead us to build a life together filled with love, trust, and countless memories.

When we got over there, it started to drizzle. We rushed to stand beneath the canopy of a jungle gym to avoid getting unnecessarily wet. Within a minute or so, it began to rain, not pouring but a little more than a drizzle. Now, that was the moment the odds were stacked in my favor. I looked at her and raised my voice over the sound of raindrops splashing against the ground, *"You can save yourself the second date and just dance with me here. This can count for the bet you lost, and then if you don't want to, you don't have to go out with me again. Fair's fair, right?"*

There was a brief pause, and somewhere nearby, the clouds thundered.

"I want to go out with you again, and I can dance with you right now."

I took out my phone, turned on the music app, and chose a Luke Bryan station because I was nervous, trying to move quickly, and his name was the first to pop up on my screen.

I prayed out loud.

"Luke Bryan, please don't fuck this up for me."

Rebecca laughed and responded.

"I'm sure he won't!"

I hoped not to mess this up. I did not want any pop or upbeat music because it would be one of our first memories together if we could make this last forever, and I wanted it to be romantic and magical for her.

It ended up playing "Roller Coaster," which was not a huge hit compared to the other songs by him at that time. Nevertheless, it was slower and had nothing to do with first love, but that became our song imprinted in our dear memory of our first date. As we started to dance, it became abundantly clear that our size difference was really fucking this dance up. We couldn't dance well together because she's 5'2" and I'm 6'3". I didn't know if it was romantic or weird at that point, but I decided to pick her up, and she wrapped her legs around me – which was more than enough approval for me.

At that moment, with our bodies swaying to the music, I held her close, feeling an indescribable connection between us. Nervous laughter filled the air as we both acknowledged the surreal and unexpected turn our date had taken. And then, our lips met, and it felt like perfect harmony.

For me, that kiss represented everything I had hoped for but had never thought possible on this date with what she teasingly called "a baby." Little did she know that this "baby" was head over heels in love with her.

We danced to one song after another, getting lost in each other's company. Kissing, talking, laughing – it all felt so natural and effortless. Our connection went beyond the physical; it was as if we had known each other for a lifetime.

As the rain started pouring, we sought shelter under a ramada and continued our heartfelt conversation. It was then that I found myself blurting out my sincere desire to marry her someday. I couldn't help but reveal my emotions because she was the one person I felt completely comfortable and open with.

I explained to her that my grandparents had a profound influence on me. Their enduring love and upcoming 50th wedding anniversary inspired me to seek a love that would last a lifetime. I wanted to grow old together, just like they did, and celebrate our 50th anniversary side by side.

Though she laughed and called me crazy, I couldn't hold back my feelings. I was determined and persistent in expressing my love and commitment to her. She had been hurt in past relationships, but I wanted to assure her that I would do anything to love and treat her in the way she truly deserved.

Despite her initial skepticism, I continued to be unwavering in my feelings and intentions. I knew deep down that she was the one I wanted to share my life with, and I was willing to do whatever it took to make her realize the depth of my love for her.

***

A few months had flown by, and I was now 23 years old when Rebecca became pregnant with our daughter. The news filled me with overwhelming joy and love. It was an incredible moment for both of us, and she graciously allowed me to choose our daughter's name. Kaiya was a name that had been dear to me since my high school days, a choice I had made and told my friend George about years ago.

Now, I have been blessed with three beautiful children, Logan and Kaiya, and Adrian, Rebecca's Son. Rebecca, despite being older than me, was the perfect partner, and I learned that age was merely a number when it came to the depth of our love and connection. We had shared complete honesty from the beginning, knowing there was nothing to lose. We envisioned a future together, getting married, and living happily ever after, committed to making it work no matter what challenges came our way.

However, there were practical considerations to address. We both had children, one from a previous relationship and the other our own. I had been transparent with Rebecca about my past, financial situation, and even the fact that my ex was still living with my parents. Despite my promise to marry her, the reality was that I wasn't financially prepared to do so.

Four years later, we found ourselves expecting again, this time with twins. With this development, Rebecca put a "shot clock" on me, expressing that she didn't want any more children out of wedlock. In response, I made a playful suggestion, half-serious, half-joking, to go to the courthouse and get married immediately.

Deep down, though, we both knew we wanted a proper wedding, surrounded by our loved ones. We began exploring various venues and vendors, considering the size of our families and the potential cost of the celebration. With both of us coming from large Mexican families, the guest list quickly added up to about 300 people, and the projected cost soared to $15,000 to $20,000.

The financial burden seemed overwhelming, and we knew that wasn't the way we wanted to start our married life. So, we decided that an extravagant wedding wasn't the right path for us. There had to be another way.

We made a conscious decision to prioritize our children's future over an extravagant wedding. We both realized that the memories and significance of a costly celebration would fade over time and instead, we opted to save up for more practical and meaningful purposes. Whether it was for their medical needs or for a special vacation just for the 7 of us, we believed it was a more sensible investment.

Our relationship was unlike any other I had experienced before, and that uniqueness carried over into our approach to marriage. We understood that marriage wasn't just about the wedding day but a commitment to ongoing work and dedication to each other. It provided a sense of security and belonging that we both cherished.

As life progressed, our roles shifted naturally. My wife began pursuing her career as a sonographer after our daughter was born, and with her increased income, it made more financial sense for me to stay home and take care of the kids.

When my twins were born, I was granted 12 weeks of paternity leave, and after that, I made the decision to quit my job and become a full-time dad for my children. Our family dynamic evolved, and our perspectives on family roles shifted accordingly. While I used to be the breadwinner when we were a family of five, my wife now took on that role when we became a family of seven. I wholeheartedly embraced my new responsibilities at home, taking care of the house, chores, and everything that involved running a household.

Our relationship exemplified the idea that family roles don't have to be fixed or conform to traditional norms. We embraced the flexibility of adapting to the changing needs of our family and supporting each other in our respective roles. Through it all, our bond grew stronger, built on mutual respect, love, and the shared goal of providing the best life for our children.

We no longer have codependency. If I were to pass away tomorrow, she would be okay, and if she were to pass away, I would be okay, too. To put it differently, we are a co-dependently independent couple. We love being around each other all the time, but we don't need to be. It's a choice, and we choose each other almost always.

Honestly, there's nothing I've ever wanted to do without her since we met, and she feels the same way from what I'm told. When we go on vacations, we do it as a group, with my kids and wife always together. We even party together. That's how we enjoy life. Some might say that the guys should go off on their own and the girls do their thing separately, but from my perspective, that's not as much fun.

The love and care we have for each other and our family define the meaning of our lives. I'm proud to say that this approach has strengthened our bond in a way I haven't seen in anyone else. That's why I'm so proud of our ability to face everything together. Technically, we both have a stepson, and we have boys and a daughter of our own. We've been single parents, raised a singleton child, and brought up identical twins together. So, it's safe to say that we've faced many obstacles as a team, and this experience has given us a wealth of parenting knowledge. It has shaped us into what I consider our version of a perfect couple (though we're not perfect parents, no matter how hard we try).

Some people might call this extreme codependency, claim it's absurd, or suggest we shouldn't be like that. But the truth is, I absolutely love what we've built together. My sole focus now is to give her and our kids the life they deserve.

This drive sustains me through my battles with depression, anxiety, and any other hardships that come my way. No matter what happens, I'll always be there for my family, just like my dad and grandfather were. It's become a family legacy, and I'm damn sure I won't be the one to break it.

Chapter 9 – Career

Whether you're embarking on your first job or contemplating a career change to venture into a new field, the mix of excitement and nerves is palpable.

My journey began at the tender age of 15 when I secured my first job. The exhilaration was undeniable as I became a barback and busboy at an upscale cowboy bar/restaurant in Tucson. It was a whole new world for me, exposing me to a different class of individuals and their professional demeanor during business meetings, friendly chats, and joking exchanges – all valuable experiences that would shape my future, considering the connections I'd make there.

My time at the restaurant was relatively brief, probably lasting no more than six to eight months. Unfortunately, I made a grave mistake and got fired for smoking weed with the sous chef. Sneaking into the freezer for a quick joint before returning to work proved to be my downfall, as a sharp-eyed bartender caught wind of it, and just like that, my job vanished.

As sports gradually took precedence in my life, transforming from a mere hobby into a central focus, I found myself spending three to four hours daily at the gym, dedicatedly practicing with my squad every day of the week. The more committed I became to sports, the harder it was to maintain focus on my second job at Hollister Co. At 17-18 years old, I wrestled with the dilemma of whether to prioritize work or pursue a career in athletics.

In the midst of my indecision, I enrolled in college. While attending classes, I also tried my hand at management at Jimmy John's, but it was short-lived. Just two months after starting college, fate dealt a cruel blow when I suffered a severe knee injury during a late-night basketball game, requiring extensive knee reconstruction. This setback rendered me unable to work or continue my studies, leaving me immobile for about four months.

Throughout that arduous period of recovery, I yearned for a return to normalcy – to run, walk, and work without hindrance. Feeling helpless and ineffective, I eagerly awaited the day when I could regain control of my life and resume my pursuits with newfound determination.

After recovering from my knee injury, I found myself without a job. It was during this time that I met Erica, the mom of my oldest son, at a party. Our relationship quickly progressed, and with her pregnancy looming, I needed to secure employment again. Thanks to a connection through my aunt, I landed a job selling cars at a large auto dealership dealing with brands Ford and Lincoln. Surprisingly, I discovered I had a knack for sales, effectively convincing people to make purchases. However, right before my son was born, I realized that being a car salesman wasn't the path I wanted to pursue, so I left the job without hesitation.

Struggling to find a fulfilling occupation with no substantial qualifications, I decided to leverage my size. It led me to become a bouncer at nightclubs, where I was exposed to an old-school mentality that dealt with violence in a rough manner. The job was fraught with danger, and I found myself in numerous life-threatening situations, from preventing stabbings to witnessing drive-bys. While I survived those two years working as a bouncer, it was an intense and harrowing experience.

Tired of the physical demands and constant risks, I transitioned to call center work, motivated by the higher pay and better hours. However, the monotonous days of sitting in a chair left me mentally drained and unfulfilled, leading me to switch call centers multiple times in a short span.

Eventually, I found myself back in the nightclub scene, where I met my future wife, who would become my best friend and lifelong soulmate. Over the next two years, I honed my skills at the same club, with me being promoted to assistant manager.

With the girls coming in and making purchases, including drinks and stage rent, we, the management staff, would receive a substantial percentage of those sales, allowing us to earn more. The standard hourly rate was $10, and I would receive 10% of everything – 10% of the bar sales, 10% of the doorman tips, and so on. In total, the management could rake in about $300-$475 a day. As a 23-year-old, that was awesome! Meanwhile, my wife, Rebecca, was pregnant with our daughter but continued working up until three days before our daughter's birth, earning between $400 and $600 per shift. Both of us were putting in at least four days a week, and financially, things were enough, leaving us content with what we were earning.

However, our contentment was short-lived as I unexpectedly got fired on Christmas Eve for something I didn't even do. It was a shocking and frustrating turn of events that left us uncertain about what lay ahead.

Thankfully, my journey didn't come to a halt there. I've always found a way to provide for my family, no matter the circumstances. After getting fired, I reached out to a guy whom I admired greatly. He had an impressive career in the MLB, making him a role model for me. I messaged him to express my curiosity about his work, confessing my lack of knowledge in insurance and finance.

Surprisingly, he invited me to visit him, and when I arrived at his office, I was awestruck by the towering building. It was a structure I'd always wanted to explore and stand atop for a bird's eye view of the city. My friend, dressed in a three-piece suit, greeted me with a warm smile. I felt a bit underdressed in jeans and a polo shirt, but he was welcoming and led me inside.

He introduced me to the world of life insurance, explaining various concepts such as licenses, mutual funds, annuities, and stocks and bonds. My knowledge in this area was close to non-existent, and I felt like a blank slate.

I have to admit I'm driven by my love for money. It might sound a bit greedy, but more than that, I don't want my kids to experience some of the same hardships I went through during my childhood. While I cherished my early years, I also faced some traumatic experiences. As a father, my ultimate goal is to shield my children from the harsh realities of the world for as long as possible.

Upon discovering the potential in the life insurance industry, I was hired promptly after a background check. It turned out that the company had set various milestones to foster healthy competition among employees. In my first year, I managed to achieve one or two milestones until I left to go to an independent firm. That was a terrible experience that would lead me to work for a company that's known for being a good neighbor.

I worked in the P&C insurance and finance industry for about two years, which brought my total experience in this field to four years. Around the same time I started my job, my wife secured a position as a sonographer, specializing in ultrasound for vascular and abdominal regions. Her job turned out to be quite lucrative, and she quickly began bringing in a substantial income. In her first year, she earned more than either of us had ever seen on a W-2, that's for sure, which was more than enough for both of us.

Our life took a turn when our twins were born, as I mentioned earlier in my story. We faced the reality that daycare expenses equaled my earnings at that time. With our daughter already in the picture, putting all three kids in daycare would have been financially burdensome. This led to a decision for me to quit my job and take on the role of the primary caregiver. It was not an easy choice, as it dealt a huge blow to my ego. While I allowed others to make jokes about the situation, privately, I confided in my wife about my anxieties and the toll it was taking on my mental health. Not being able to provide for my family caused severe depression, but my wife and I had open discussions about our roles and responsibilities.

Thus began my 1st phase as a househusband. I stayed at home to care for the twins until they turned two. This meant taking care of everything – cooking, cleaning, changing diapers, and handling school drop-offs and pick-ups. Spending around four hours a day in the car for these tasks was exhausting, but I embraced my responsibilities to the best of my ability. Our twins were quite active and challenging to manage, adding an extra layer of difficulty.

Once the twins were old enough and my wife's additional pay raise made daycare more affordable, I decided to rejoin the club where my wife and I initially met. It felt like familiar territory, and I got hired in a management position.

During the next nine months of working at the club, I found myself spending less and less time with my family. The demands of the job required me to work Friday and Saturday nights, as we were understaffed and needed more doormen. Consequently, my responsibilities multiplied as I ran around, serving customers, fetching bottles, and handling more tasks. Additionally, the absence of my boss, the club's GM, from Sundays to Tuesdays burdened me with even more responsibilities.

As time went on, matters worsened. We struggled to find people to work with, and customer attendance declined. Despite numerous promises, no actions were taken by the owner or the authorities to rectify the situation. Compounding the issue, the other GM began engaging in illegal dealings, putting everyone at risk, including the club's reputation and liquor license. Worried about the potential consequences and unwilling to have my reputation tarnished by association, I decided to take action.

I reached out to the vice president of the club, detailing all my issues and concerns. He was surprised that we hadn't connected earlier, realizing that there were better opportunities for me within the club, such as a GM position or even a chance to manage another club in a different city. He held me in high regard because of the respect I showed everyone, protecting my coworkers from disrespect and creating a positive work environment. This quality impressed the vice president, and he offered me the opportunity to manage a club in a city of my choosing.

While the offer boosted my ego, I made a different decision. I decided to explore other opportunities and gracefully left the club on good terms.

Chapter 10 – Twins

Having twins brings numerous benefits and joys, but it also comes with unique challenges for parents. Responsibilities and expenses double, creating a whole new set of circumstances to navigate. When my wife, a sonographer, discovered we were having twins through an ultrasound at home, we were both shocked and excited.

At first, I thought she was joking when she exclaimed, 'It's twins!' I was lying lazily on the couch and couldn't believe what she was saying. But when I saw the two cells on the screen, I realized she wasn't kidding. We had two babies on the way.

The news of having twins took some time to sink in, and we had serious conversations about whether we could handle it. There was a moment when we considered other options, but being Catholic, it didn't sit well with us. After some contemplation, we decided to embrace the journey of raising twins, even though we knew it would be challenging.

As the appointments progressed, we discovered that the twins would be identical, adding another layer of hilarity to the situation. We joked about how we wouldn't be able to tell them apart, anticipating the fun and confusion they would bring into our lives.

However, along with the excitement, anxiety crept in. We were aware of the higher mortality rate for twins, especially as my wife was thirty-four at that point, which posed additional risks. The likelihood of losing one or both of the twins was a significant concern, especially since we had already experienced a miscarriage in the past.

Despite the apprehensions, we remained hopeful and committed to providing the best care and love for our twins, embracing the unique journey that lay ahead for our family.

As a practical couple, my wife and I were well aware of the odds and potential risks, given our previous experiences with miscarriages. To keep a low profile about the pregnancies, we decided not to share the news until we reached the second trimester.

Before informing my parents, we knew we couldn't hide the fact that Rebecca was expecting twins for long. With two babies on the way, her belly would grow significantly within a short period. So, we decided to break the news to my parents, who lived just a few miles away from us.

The moment is etched in my memory when I shared the news during one of my son's soccer practices. Rebecca chose not to go because she thought that my parents might not have the best outlook.

As I asked my mom, "Hey, can I tell you something?" she playfully responded, "Rebecca's pregnant," knowing that was my usual way of sharing such announcements.

"Yeah! How'd you know?" I asked, momentarily surprised that she might have gotten the whiff of it.

"I didn't, but that is the only way you've ever told me."

I smiled and said, "Okay, but you want to hear the kicker?"

"What?" She asked, frowning.

"It's fucking identical twins."

My dad laughed loudly and said, "You're fucking lying."

I pulled out the ultrasound pictures from my pocket and handed it to him, "They're gonna look exactly the same. If they are anything like Logan, they'll fucking look just like me."

My dad laughed again. Well, he took it way better than my mom did. She did not necessarily have bad feelings, either. When I told her, she wished me good luck.

"Thanks! I'm gonna need it." I said.

While my dad shifted the mood to a lighter atmosphere, he made jokes like, "Oh, well, let's name them Steve and Todd!"

My dad bought them Christmas stockings that year with an S and T.

When I added that they were identical twins, my dad found it hard to believe. I showed them the ultrasound, and the reality of a pair of identical twins started to sink in.

Despite the excitement, we knew the situation was becoming riskier. Losing the twins would be devastating for us, given the high-risk nature of the pregnancy. However, we laughed and joked around to keep the atmosphere light.

As the time for delivery approached, we faced increasing anxiety. The high-risk factor was already daunting, and we were concerned about the potential challenges ahead. During the delivery preparations, we encountered a rather difficult anesthesiologist who lacked any bedside manner, but we remained focused on the task at hand.

Witnessing both cesarean and natural births in the past, I felt well-prepared for the delivery of my twins. It was like completing a parenting bingo card, having experienced various aspects of pregnancy and childbirth with my previous children.

During the twins' C-section, I was by my wife's side on the operating table, where they had set up a clear plastic screen for her to see, but her mind was numb, and she couldn't focus. The anesthesiologist, unfortunately, gave off a negative vibe right from the start and lacked good bedside manners, unlike the excellent ones we had for my first two babies.

As they pulled out the first baby, we had to wait for a sixty-second period as twins cannot be born in the same minute, apparently. But in our case, they were ready to be born within the first minute of the C-section. We waited around forty seconds after the first baby. The medical team kept a close eye on the clock to ensure timely delivery.

During this time, I noticed a significant amount of blood on the floor, about 12 inches in diameter. I chose not to mention it to my wife to avoid alarming her. Instead, I tried to get the attention of the anesthesiologist, who was sitting across from the operating table in a chair. I called his name about two or three times, but he didn't turn around. So I patted him on the shoulder and whispered, "Hey, can you fucking look at the floor for a second. You have to see the blood loss that she's having."

Then he looked down and blurted out, "Oh, shit!" He then returned to his computer and began changing things because I understood that he may have dropped the ball at some point. Her blood loss may have affected her capacity to enter and exit consciousness. Because it was his area of expertise, he had to pay close attention to every detail.

In such critical moments, every second counts, and it was essential for the medical team to be vigilant and responsive to ensure a safe delivery for both my wife and the twins.

In moments of duress or crisis, I've always excelled at staying positive and calm, a trait I believe I inherited from my mom. I understood the importance of holding it together to prevent others from panicking. When my wife was in the operating room for the delivery of our twins, I kept my composure and assured her that everything would be fine.

After the babies were taken to the other side of the birthing suite, I briefly left my wife to go and check on them. I wanted to ensure I knew which one was baby A and baby B so I wouldn't mix them up. I reassured her that she was going to be okay and expressed my love before leaving her side.

Reflecting on that moment during a recent conversation, my wife asked me what I would have done if something had happened to her during childbirth. I tried to make a light-hearted joke, but she knew it was a tough question. I admitted that I wouldn't know how to handle such a tragedy and how incredibly thankful I was that it didn't happen.

We had discussed similar scenarios before, contemplating what we would do if one of us passed away unexpectedly. While we both claimed to have plans and to be ready to keep moving, the reality of such a situation would have been overwhelmingly horrible.

With five kids to take care of, including the twins, I made the decision to leave my job at the insurance agency three months after their birth. Rebecca had to return to work once the twins turned three months old, and it was essential for me to be there for our growing family.

Navigating the challenges of being a stay-at-home father while my wife returned to work was undeniably tough, both physically and emotionally. It wasn't a role I had envisioned for myself or for her, but it was something we had to do for the sake of our growing family. Taking care of five children, including two infants, was like juggling bowls of water, but it was a responsibility I couldn't avoid.

Despite my initial doubts about being good in this role, I found that spending more quality time with my kids than my wife could have unexpected benefits. It strengthened our relationship as we gained a deeper understanding and respect for each other's roles. We had experienced both sides—her being a stay-at-home mom and me stepping into a traditional man's role to support the household and vice-versa. These circumstances forced us to see things from each other's perspective, creating a profound mutual understanding.

While we had our occasional disagreements, they were usually small arguments that we quickly resolved. We never crossed the line of utter disrespect or name-calling. Even in the most heated moments, we were able to talk it out and move forward, nurturing our relationship.

During those three years, our lives have seen significant changes. I went back to work at the club, and my wife has made remarkable progress in her field. Her success has allowed us to experience things that many couples may not have had the opportunity to do in 2020. Living in Arizona, which isn't the cheapest place to live, surely not the most expensive, we made the decision to move in with my parents to save money for our future home.

Our priority was to save up for a house after the twins were born. Living with my parents was a temporary measure to achieve this goal. It was a necessary sacrifice to secure a better future for our family. Then, in 2020, we bought our house.

Having achieved our goal of buying a house, we turned it into something we can truly call our own. I dedicated countless hours to renovating and transforming the house into a place of love and comfort for our family of five. From building a porch to making the furniture, painting the walls, hanging artwork, and framing pictures, every detail was carefully thought out to create a space where we could all feel happy and at ease.

The hard work and effort have paid off, and our children have taken to the house with joy and excitement. They enjoy exploring every corner, and it warms our hearts to see them happy in their own little world. The house has become a place of laughter, growth, and beautiful memories.

As we settle into our new home, we look back at our journey together with pride and gratitude. From facing challenges as parents to working hard to achieve our dreams, we have grown stronger as a couple and as a family. Our home is a symbol of our love, dedication, and commitment to providing the best life possible for our children.

Looking around the house now, I feel a sense of fulfillment. The walls echo with the laughter and footsteps of our children, and the rooms are filled with the warmth of our love. This house is not just a place to live; it is a reflection of our journey together—a place where love and happiness thrive.

Our story continues, and we face each day with the same determination and love that brought us to this point. As a family, we will continue to cherish every moment, celebrate our accomplishments, and overcome any challenges that may come our way. Our home is a testament to the life we have built together, and we are excited for the many adventures that lie ahead.

Chapter 11 – DNA

The decision to do a DNA test started with my playful jokes about our kids not being mine. My wife would always humorously respond by offering to get the DNA test done to put an end to my teasing. Over the years, I had also been curious about my own ethnicity and heritage, so I agreed to the test, knowing it would answer both questions.

The results came back after a few weeks, and I wasn't surprised by mine, as I had expected to see some unknown connections due to my non-biological relationship with my father, Chris.

However, the revelation was shocking for my wife. She discovered that her biological father was not the man who had raised her. Her dad, who had since passed away, meant everything to her, and this newfound information left her reeling.

Growing up, my wife and her sister didn't resemble each other much, but they never suspected that they were half-sisters. It turned out that her mom had a one-night stand during a separation from her father, resulting in Rebecca's conception. Even when her mom came back into her life, she never mentioned it. Who would?

The discovery of her biological father led us to connect with him. It took some time to track him down, but when we finally met him for dinner, it opened up a new chapter in our lives. We maintain a relationship with him, meeting regularly for dinners and even visiting him in Mexico.

He was an enjoyable and fun person, but we realized that he might not have been the best father figure for Rebecca as he was more of the "party guy." Nevertheless, the connection was undeniable, and we could see the resemblance between Rebecca and her biological family in photographs and in person.

Finding her biological father not only unveiled a new part of Rebecca's identity but also brought a sense of closure to the unanswered questions from her past. Despite the surprising turn of events, we embraced the new connection and welcomed her biological father into our lives, cherishing the bond that was formed between them.

When I received my results, a list of relatives I recognized, including first cousins, second cousins, and third cousins, appeared before me. However, there was something odd about my tree. The name under the family/siblings category stunned me – Anthony Osborn. Instantly, my mind raced, concluding that Kyle must have a son he didn't know about. I wasted no time and messaged this man named Charles, or Tony as he preferred to be called, on every social platform I could find. I believed him to be my half-brother.

However, my attempts to reach him went unanswered, leaving me bewildered and frustrated. When I explored his page on the family tree, it displayed only his grandfather, mom, and himself, a single straight line that left me comparing it to my own fully-filled family tree. The obsession I had developed over my lineage now seemed trivial compared to this newfound revelation.

Desperate for a response, I messaged him again, offering to reveal the identity of his father if he wished to know. Still, silence. As that night wore on, around nine o'clock, I found myself at work in the club, unable to shake this perplexing revelation from my mind. I decided to call my mom, seeking answers to this enigmatic puzzle.

"Mom," I asked, trying to remain composed, "does the name Anthony Osborn mean anything to you? Do you know anyone with that last name?"

She replied, "No, I can't recall anyone with that name."

"I'm pretty sure I have a half-brother, and his name is Charles. I thought maybe he's connected to someone in your circle, like someone who might have had a relationship with Kyle or something like that."

Her response was a brief pause before she said, "I don't know anyone with that last name. What's his birthday?"

"January 23," I answered. "He's just twenty days older than me."

With genuine uncertainty, she replied, "I have no idea. I can look through some old yearbooks or ask around for anyone with the last name Osborn."

Feeling disheartened, I said, "Alright, I thought you might know."

The conversation left me with more questions than answers, and the mysterious Anthony Osborn continued to elude me, evoking a deep sense of intrigue and wonder as to the secret that lay beneath the surface of my family's history.

The next morning, still haunted by the revelations from the previous night, I couldn't wait any longer. I called Kyle around nine in the morning, hoping he could shed some light on the mysterious Charles.

"Kyle, I need to ask you something," I began.

"Yeah?" he replied.

"Before you went to prison, did you have any other relationships? I mean, did you sleep with anyone?"

He hesitated for a moment before answering, "Not until that point. Your mom was the only one, except for one night when I cheated and felt terrible about it."

My heart raced as I continued, "Well, there's this guy, Charles, showing up on my ancestry results."

"Holy shit!" Kyle exclaimed, recognizing the name. "I think that's Mandy's name. Rick's chick from high school!"

Confused, I inquired, "What do you mean?"

He explained, "There was this girl I hooked up with, but we never went all the way, so I don't think it's her."

Realization struck me, and I shared my thoughts, "So, there are two possibilities: Either Anthony and I are both yours, or Anthony and I are both Rick's."

Without hesitation, Kyle suggested, "Hold on, let me call Rick."

Moments later, Kyle came back to our call. He confirmed that Anthony was indeed his son.

It all fell into place in my mind, and I uttered in disbelief.

"FUCK!"

With this revelation, I knew that Paige was Rick's daughter. She had always known about her brother, Tony, but he was never brought up/around, but my mind couldn't handle the chaos. I erupted into a frenzy, shouting, "WHAT BULLSHIT IS THIS?" The reality of our situation hit me like a ton of bricks; I couldn't bear the disgust I felt toward myself and the situation we all just found ourselves in.

Losing control of my emotions, I began to have an emotional and existential breakdown. My faith in God, my life, everything seemed to crumble before my eyes, leaving me questioning how I had ended up in such a nightmarish scenario.

Waiting for Rebecca to return home, I knew I had to share this with her. I mustered the courage and told her that I had finally found out who my real father was.

The shock in Rebecca's eyes was evident as she asked, "What? Real father? Whose Rick?"

I mustered the courage to respond, "Rick. He's my real father. That means I've slept with my sister. I can't believe I had a relationship with my own sister for a year and a half. I feel sick."

On that day, my mom and grandma were at the hospital, there to support my aunt during a medical procedure. I decided to go there, but before leaving, I made a quick stop at my parent's house to drop off a few things. Dad was home at the time.

I shared with him, "I need to tell Mom something fucking crazy. I can't tell you right now because I have to tell her first. I promise I'll talk to you about it later."

Understanding the need for privacy, he agreed to wait.

As I drove to the hospital, only a few minutes away, I called my mom and asked if we could talk in private. However, she insisted I come upstairs since it was just her and my grandma.

Reluctantly, I complied and greeted them both. However, with the hospital staff absent from the waiting room, I knew I had to share the truth quickly before anyone came back.

So, standing there between my mom and grandma, I looked at my mom sternly and spoke plainly, "Kyle's not my dad. It's Rick, which means I messed with my sister for a year and a half!"

An uncomfortable silence enveloped the room, leaving us all stunned by the gravity of the revelation.

As my mom and I struggled to keep our emotions in check, tears rolled down my cheeks. The whirlwind of feelings inside my head was overwhelming, and I couldn't comprehend the situation. I felt betrayed by my mom, who had always emphasized the importance of honesty.

Reflecting on my own life as a parent, I acknowledged that I had been wild when I was younger and that there might be more children out there who are biologically mine. However, I vowed never to lie to my kids about their birth and identity.

We went downstairs to continue our conversation, and my mom shared that she remembered the night it happened, but alcohol had clouded most of her memories. I'm told Rick had taken advantage of her when she was drunk, resulting in her pregnancy. She felt immense guilt and embarrassment, even as I was writing this book. I never intended to shame anyone, but I realized that my discovery has deeply affected my mom and everyone else involved with this story.

In the midst of this emotional turmoil, I reached out to Tony on Facebook, and we bonded over some dark humor about the irony of our situation. Although we had never met, we only lived one neighborhood apart. Life had played a cruel joke by keeping us apart.

Despite the strange circumstances, I felt a genuine desire to get to know Tony. We chatted for a good 30–40 minutes before inviting him over for a barbecue at my place. The weekend turned out to be quite eventful, as Rebecca's biological father had visited on Friday, and Tony and his girlfriend came over on Saturday. It was an overwhelming but oddly fulfilling experience.

Before this revelation, I had always believed that I had daddy issues, but now, my family dynamics have become even more intricate. I now had three fathers: Kyle, who had always wanted to be there for me; Chris, who never failed to be the dad I needed; and now Rick, my biological father.

Despite waiting for Rick to reach out, he seemed strangely distant. After a month had passed, I finally received a friend request from him on Facebook. However, it was annoyingly ambiguous since he and his wife shared the account, leaving me uncertain about who sent the request. The situation only added to the complexity of our newly found relationships.

At this time, I reached out to Paige on the ancestry app, "Hey, if you're up for a talk, let me know when you have time. I imagine you feel the same as me."

She texted back, "To be honest, I'm having a lot of issues about it. We had no idea we were related. We genuinely thought you were Kyle's and I was Rick's. So, at that time, neither of us thought there would be anything wrong with it. We can't change the past, and it happened. On the other hand, we're finding out at 30 that we're siblings, and that's pretty fucked up. Really, I want to pretend it never happened. If you want to build a relationship with us as our brother, I'm okay with it as long as we never mention anything of our past. I know Rick feels guilty, though, and he would like to build a relationship with you."

I did not feel good about the idea of a relationship at all, so I replied, "I understand that completely. But to be honest, he and my mom are in the wrong here, so he can reach out whenever he sees fit. I see no need to try to become a part of your family. Not to be rude, but at this age, what can he do for me? I say we can keep things away the way they are for now. If anyone in your family reaches out, I'm always happy to answer any questions or anything like that."

She responded with "Yeah," and I believe he knew about it because she was speaking for him. I told her that he could reach out whenever he wanted to try to make amends or at least say something like, "Hey, this fucking crazy, right."

She replied, "He feels really shitty about his and your mom's teenage stupidity and for the fact that he has another son that he didn't know about for 30 years."

"He might not want a relationship at this point because he has lived his whole life not knowing, and he had been fine." I texted back.

Her reply popped up, "He said that he requested to be your friend on Facebook, so he does want a chance to talk to you as well."

I told her, "And I did not see fit to respond to that message. Sending a friend request to somebody on Facebook isn't making an effort. It is not like owning up to your issues. It's not valid."

Meeting Tony and learning more about Rick was both enlightening and disappointing. Tony, working in the oilfield, made it challenging to meet frequently, but whenever he was home, we tried to get together at least once or twice. He warned me not to expect much from Rick, as he had been a terrible father figure to Tony.

"I don't expect anything from anyone," I told Tony, sharing my defense mechanism of never setting high expectations to avoid disappointment. My dark view of the world had taught me that everyone was out to deceive or harm me.

I already had a strong relationship with the person I thought was my dad, Kyle, who had always said he looked out for me. Now, after learning the truth about my paternity, I struggled to accept anything from Rick, especially since he hadn't taken care of Tony.

Tony shared a small but significant incident where he had waved at Rick while he was riding his bike through the neighborhood, but Rick ignored him and continued on his way. It seemed that he wanted nothing to do with Tony, possibly because he didn't consider him someone to be proud of or he disliked how Tony represented him.

"He hates my mom," Tony confided in frustration, "All he does is talk shit about her."

I couldn't help but think, 'What an asshole.'

Tony's mom, Mandy, had been only fifteen when Rick got her pregnant, and two weeks later, he got my mom pregnant when she was nineteen. The whole situation was a mess, and it had been embarrassing for his mom as well.

Amidst this chaos, I found solace in my mother-in-law's support and understanding. She had gone through her own challenges recently with everything having to do with Rebecca, but she was there for me during the first month and after discovering the truth. She provided a non-judgmental ear and offered support for both my wife and me as we navigated this new reality. She visited us frequently, showing her care and love during this life-shattering time in our lives.

The weight of my secret was too heavy, and nobody in my family wanted to talk about it, mainly because of my dark sense of humor. I coped with the situation by making terrible jokes, saying the most vile and disgusting things to grab everyone's attention and force them to address the truth. I refused to let anyone walk on eggshells around me, wanting everyone to face reality together and find humor in it. Over the last three years since this revelation, I became okay with people making fun of me, as I had already made jokes about it myself.

Although I felt ashamed, I had learned to live with it and no longer wanted to speak about it. I never wanted to embarrass my mom or anyone else, but it seemed like nobody else in the family was willing to help except for my wife's mom, Rose. Eventually, I gathered the courage to sit across the table from my mom and assure her that I wasn't mad at her. I had no problem expressing my anger or frustration to her when needed, so it was unfair to assume that I harbored resentment. I understood that people make mistakes, and I had already forgiven her, reiterating this point countless times.

With empathy and appreciation for my mom's sacrifices, I expressed, "You're my mom, and I understand. I've had a great life, and it wouldn't have been this way if you had chosen Rick. I'm thankful for everything you've done for me."

My main concern, however, was the incestuous aspect of the situation. It tore at my soul, making me seek out new religions that could potentially absolve such a sin. I consulted with priests and bishops, and most of them agreed that I could find forgiveness through penance and atonement, knowing that I was innocent because we didn't know. They assured me that my conscience was cleared once I acknowledged the sin and realized its gravity.

Although I managed to put these thoughts at bay over time, they still haunt me occasionally, creeping into my mind and unsettling me. Yet, my ultimate desire was for my mom to reach out to me to ask about my well-being, emotions, and experiences. However, every time I wondered if there was anything she could do, the answer was always 'No.'

I hesitated to voice these thoughts out loud, fearing that it would make them more real and intensify my shame. But during our conversation, seeing the guilt on my mom's face made me realize that I needed to stop dwelling on the past and berating myself.

With a sense of finality, I thought to myself, "All right, it's time to stop beating a dead horse at this point."

Epilogue – Today and Tomorrow

Despite his friend request on Facebook, I can't shake the feeling that his wife might have been the one behind it. Paige, too, hasn't made any further contact after our messages on the ancestry app. Tony and I have discussed the possibility of going to see Rick in person to confront him and seek answers, but we're still weighing our options.

It's clear that Rick needs to be held accountable for his actions, especially since Paige seems adamant about avoiding the subject altogether. I don't know their family anymore, but I guess their lives continue. However, I believe it's essential to address the situation and eventually find closure.

On the other hand, the bond with Rebecca's biological father is growing stronger, and we're making plans for vacations and trips together. I've also grown closer to Rebecca's mom, who has become another pillar of support in my life.

As for my own mom, the healing conversations we've had have brought us closer together. She now will hopefully understand that I harbor no resentment toward her, and our relationship has significantly improved.

My dad, Chris, and I have developed a friendship as well. While I still admire him for his leadership and seek his guidance, we now connect on a more personal level, which has improved our dynamic.

As for Kyle, the revelation about my biological father seems to have taken a toll on his friendship. He and Rick were once best friends, but it appears that the gravity of the situation may have strained their relationship. I'm unsure of Rick's perspective, as he hasn't reached out to Kyle, and Kyle hasn't attempted to contact Rick either, to my knowledge.

In Tony, I have found a brother. We spend quality time together, hanging out and having barbecues. Our bond as brothers has brought us joy and fulfillment, and we both cherish the unexpected gift of brotherhood. It's a testament to how life's twists and turns can lead to unexpected blessings.

My children are aware of my newfound family connections, although I have shielded them from the full details. They know they have a new uncle and me, a new biological father somewhere out there. We even did DNA tests for them to ensure they had clarity about their heritage. Fortunately, the results confirmed that all the kids that were supposed to be mine were indeed mine, providing a sense of relief and closure for us all.

Rebecca and I have grown even closer through this challenging time, supporting each other through our respective journeys. We've been each other's pillars of strength during the turmoil, solidifying our bond as a couple. The experience has revealed the strength of the relationships in my life, highlighting the ones that truly matter.

Though the discovery brought its share of lessons, both enlightening and challenging, I am grateful for the insight it has provided. Life's mysteries have a way of unfolding in unexpected ways, and I've learned to embrace the journey, even in its most difficult moments.

As I close this book, I can't help but reflect on the saying, "Everything happens for a reason." Though I may not have all the answers, I am determined to move forward with courage and the knowledge that life's twists and turns have shaped me into the person I am today. I will cherish the blessings and continue to navigate the uncertainties with an open heart and an unwavering spirit.

Acknowledgments

Completing this book is a significant achievement, and I wish to express my sincere gratitude to those who have played a pivotal role in its realization. The process of bringing these words to life has encompassed both challenges and triumphs, and I am deeply appreciative of the individuals who have stood by, supported, and encouraged me throughout.

I extend my heartfelt appreciation to my wife, whose unwavering support and understanding during the creation of what I consider a most intricate narrative has been a guiding light. Her presence has provided solace during moments of uncertainty, and her belief in my abilities has served as a well of inspiration.

To my mom, your strength and determination have been a motivator since childhood. This journey has been a somewhat shared endeavor, a testament to the enduring bond we share. I extend my heartfelt gratitude for navigating challenges side by side, for sharing in both moments of triumph and failure, and for being the bedrock upon which the foundation of this book is firmly established.

My father's wise guidance and constant encouragement have formed a cornerstone for my aspirations. His firm belief in my abilities has given me the drive to pursue this creative path, and I hold a special appreciation for the invaluable life lessons he has shared.

To my grandfather, Papa, your enduring presence and love have empowered me to strive for excellence. Your roles as confidant, mentor, and, most importantly, friend have played a crucial part in shaping my journey and contributed significantly to the man I am today.

Mema, your faith in me and consistent words of motivation have been a driving force throughout my journey as a writer. Your support has propelled me beyond my perceived limitations, and I express a significant amount of gratitude for your role in my creative journey and upbringing.

To my best friend, George, you've been integral to my life. Your friendship has breathed life into my character and experiences, and I extend my sincerest appreciation for your brotherhood and loyalty throughout all these years.

Marisol, your moral compass and support were fantastic guides during moments of uncertainty in my childhood. Your guidance has led all of us through a labyrinth of creativity.

Zach, my oldest friend, your companionship through my various life stages has exemplified the enduring power of authentic friendship. Your consistent support and unwavering presence have been a source of comfort, for which I am greatly appreciative.

To each individual mentioned and those not named, your influence on my creative journey has been profound. The collective impact of your encouragement, support, and love is immeasurable, and I carry it with gratitude.

In conclusion, I extend heartfelt appreciation to all readers, friends, and supporters and to those who have embarked on this literary voyage with me.

With deep appreciation,

Cody

* 9 7 9 8 3 3 0 6 8 5 7 8 3 *